CW00363134

The Greater
by
Oswald Mosley

The Greater Britain
by
Oswald Mosley

Copyright © 2012 Black House Publishing Ltd
Printed by kind permission of the Friends of Oswald Mosley
and the Mosley Estate.

All rights reserved. No part of this book may be reproduced
in any form by any electronic or mechanical means including
photocopying, recording, or information storage and retrieval
without permission in writing from the publisher.

ISBN-13: 978-1-908476-76-0

Black House Publishing Ltd
78 York Street
London
W1H 1DP

www.blackhousepublishing.co.uk
Email: info@blackhousepublishing.co.uk

The Fasces

The fasces are the emblem which founded the power,
authority and unity of Imperial Rome. From the Rome of the past
was derived the tradition of civilisation and progress during the
past two thousand years, of which the British Empire is now the
chief custodian. The bundle of sticks symbolises the strength of
unity. Divided, they may be broken; united, they are invincible.
The axe symbolises the supreme authority of the organised State,
to which every section and faction owes allegiance.

Preface

It is now eighteen months since this book was first published, but it has not been necessary materially to revise it for a new edition. Some new facts and new developments of our detailed policy have been included. In particular the structure of Fascist Government has been defined with greater precision than in the original book. But the main argument and policy remains unaltered. Subsequent circumstances have combined to strengthen the argument and to support the policy. In the economic chapters it has scarcely been necessary to make any alteration at all. The analysis which I first advanced in my speech of resignation from the Labour Government in may 1930 is now very widely accepted, although at the time it was regarded as unorthodox, if not fantastic. In particular, the fallacy of seeking to cure unemployment solely through a revival of export trade is now almost entirely discredited.

The Economic policy, too, now finds a far wider acceptance, but only a very partial application. Some of it has been applied in America under President Roosevelt's attempt to revive industry in the far easier conditions of that country without the overriding energy and authority of an organised Fascist Movement behind him.

The policy of this book is also reflected in the recent attempts of several countries to constitute what are now called "Autarchic" organisations which I originally described as National "Insulation." It is also reflected in recent speeches and writings in this country which attempt to persuade the Old Parties to abandon the old policies from which the logic of events is driving them.

Half-hearted and partial attempts to apply a policy with reluctance under the stress of necessity are seldom successful. Nettles which are not grasped are liable to sting. Recent events only confirm the original contention of this book that in face of the grave problems which confront this country Fascism without Fascists will not work. The task before us is nothing less than the creation of a new civilisation. Before we can really begin that task we must create a new spirit. The Old Parties may imitate in belated and ineffective fashion our policies; they can never imitate or acquire our spirit. This is the supreme mission of Fascism in the world to create a revival in the spirit of man which is prerequisite to a revival in material environment. In the brief space of eighteen months that spirit has been created in Britain. The fury with which it has been assailed was anticipated in the original Introduction and Conclusion of this book, which I have left practically untouched to afford at least a proof that we knew what we were doing.

We anticipated the bitterness of the opposition we should evoke; we could not anticipate the full measure of the support we should secure. The publication of this book launched a hazardous adventure on an uncharted sea. The outcome depended upon the will and determination that remained to the British people. Our great confidence has been justified to a greater extent than we could have dared to hope. In eighteen months a small handful has grown to a mighty organisation stretching through the length and breadth of the land.

In this early period of Fascism in Britain we have advanced far more rapidly than any other Fascist movement in the world. Great struggles await us and from time to time in the future as in the past no doubt we shall experience our reverses. These things do not matter. What does matter is that a spirit has been created in Britain which in the end cannot fail. The inspiration of the spirit of Fascism eludes the description of the written word but today in Britain it is a vital fact which is felt and lived by thousands.

Thousands of men and women have dedicated themselves with selfless determination and sublime passion to the salvation of this land. A religious enthusiasm carries forward the creed of the modern world to predestined triumph. These are the realities of Fascist civilisation, for Fascism is a thing of the spirit. It is the acceptance of new values and of a new morality in a higher and nobler conception of the universe. The individual in his fusion with the ideal of service finds a greater personality and purpose. The corporate entity of Fascism embodies the finest aspirations of the human mind and spirit in superb sacrifice to a sacred purpose.

In an age of decadence and disillusion when all old values fail, the new flame purifies and inspires to loftier ambitions and mightier ends. The achievements of Fascism will be many in Britain, but the greatest has already been accomplished although the effects cannot yet be measured in terms of national policy. The spirit lives; the rest will follow.

Book 1 : Fascism and the State

IN Great Britain during the past ten years there have never been less than a million unemployed, and recently unemployment has fluctuated over a two million figure, which does not include a very large number of salaried and uninsured men and women at present unemployed. In 1929 a year which is now regarded as the peak of industrial prosperity British trade was slack, large industrial areas were almost derelict, and only the stock markets enjoyed a semblance of boom conditions.

We have tragic proof that economic life has outgrown our political institutions. Britain has failed to recover from the War period; and this result, however complicated by special causes, is largely due to a system of Government designed by, and for, the nineteenth century. Setting aside any complaint of the conduct or capacity of individual Governments, I believe that, under the existing system, Government cannot be efficiently conducted.

The object of this book is to prove, by analysis of the present situation and by constructive policy, that the necessity for a fundamental change exists. Our political system dates substantially from 1832. The intervening century has seen the invention and development of telegraph, telephone and wireless. At the beginning of the period, railways were a novelty, and a journey of a dozen miles was a serious undertaking.

Since then, railway transport has risen and prospered, only to yield place to the still greater revolution of motor transport on modern roads. The whole question of power production is less than a century old, and electricity is a recent development. The modern processes of mass production and rationalisation date only from the War period. Within the last century science has multiplied by many times the power of man to produce. Banking, as we know it today, did not exist in 1832; even the Charter of the Bank of England and the modern Gold Standard are less than a century old. Social opinion has developed almost as rapidly as economic possibilities. Well within the last century children worked twelve hours daily in mines and workshops. Men were transported for picking pockets, and hanged for stealing sheep. Leisure and education have enormously widened the public interest in matters of Government concern. The huge expansion of commerce has made us depend more and more on one another; the building-up of popular newspapers has organised and formulated popular opinion.

From the standpoint of a century ago, all these changes are revolutionary. The sphere of government has widened and the complications of government have increased. It is hardly surprising that the political system of 1832 is wholly out of date today. "The worst danger of the modern world," writes Sir Arthur Salter in his brilliant book Recovery, "is that the specialised activities of man will outrun his capacity for regulative wisdom."

Our problem is to reconcile the revolutionary changes of science with our system of government, and to harmonise individual initiative with the wider interests of the nation. Most men desire to work for themselves; laws are oppressive if they prevent people from doing so. But there is no room for interests which are not in the State's interests; laws are futile if they allow such things to be. Wise laws, and wise institutions, are those which harness without restricting; which allow human activity full play, but guide it into channels which serve the nation's ends.

FASCISM - THE MODERN MOVEMENT.

Hence the need for a New Movement, not only in politics, but in the whole of our national life. The movement is Fascist, (i) because it is based on a high conception of citizenship - ideals as lofty as those which inspired the reformers of a hundred years ago: (ii) because it recognises the necessity for an authoritative state, above party and sectional interests. Some may be prejudiced by the use of the word "Fascist," because that word has so far been completely misunderstood in this country. It would be easy for us to avoid that prejudice by using another word, but it would not be honest to do so. We seek to organise the Modern Movement in this country by British methods in a form which is suitable to and characteristic of Great Britain. We are essentially a national movement, and if our policy could be summarised in two words, they would be "Britain First". Nevertheless, the Modern Movement is by no means confined to Great Britain; it comes to all the great countries in turn as their hour of crisis approaches, and in each country it naturally assumes a form and a character suited to that nation. As a world-wide movement, it has come to be known as Fascism, and it is therefore right to use that name. If our crisis had been among the first, instead of among the last, Fascism would have been a British invention. As it is, our task is not to invent Fascism, but to find for it in Britain its highest expression and development.

Fascism does not differ from the older political movements in being a world-wide creed. Each of the great political faiths in its turn has been a universal movement: Conservatism, Liberalism and Socialism are common to nearly every country. An Englishman who calls himself a Conservative or a Liberal is not thereby adopting a foreign creed merely because foreign political parties bear the same name. He is seeking to advance, by English method and in English forms, a political philosophy which can be found in an organised form in all nations.

In this respect the Fascist occupies precisely the same position: his creed is also a world-wide faith. However, by very reason of the national nature of his policy, he must seek in the method and form of his organisation a character which is more distinctively British than the older political movements. Quite independently, we originally devised a policy for British needs of a very national character. In the development of that policy, and of a permanent political philosophy, we have reached conclusions which can only be properly described as Fascism.

MISREPRESENTATION

All new movements are misunderstood. Our British Union of Fascists will without a doubt be misrepresented by politicians of the elder schools. The movement did not begin with the wiseacres and the theorists. It was born in a surging discontent with a regime where nothing can be achieved. The Old Gang hold the stage; and, to them, misrepresentation is the path of their own salvation.

Such tactics may delay, but they cannot prevent, the advance of the movement. Nevertheless, every incident in every brutal struggle, in countries of completely different temperament and character, will be used against us. We are also faced by the fact that a few people have misused the name "Fascism" in this country, and from ignorance or in perversion have represented it as the "White Guard of reaction."

This is indeed a strange perversion of a creed of dynamic change and progress. In all countries, Fascism has been led by men who came from the "Left," and the rank and file has combined the Conservative and patriotic elements of the nation with ex-Socialists, ex-Communists and revolutionaries who have forsaken their various illusions of progress for the new and orderly reality of progress. In our new organisation we now combine within our ranks all those elements in this country who have long studied and understood the great constructive mission of Fascism; but we have no place for those who have sought to make Fascism the lackey of reaction, and have thereby represented its policy and dissipated its strength. In fact Fascism is the greatest constructive and revolutionary creed in the world. It seeks to achieve its aim legally and constitutionally, by methods of law and order; but in objective it is revolutionary or it is nothing. It challenges the existing order and advances the constructive alternative of the Corporate State. To many of us this creed represents the thing which we have sought throughout our political lives. It combines the dynamic urge to change and progress with the authority, the discipline and the order without which nothing great can be achieved.

This conception we have sought through many vicissitudes of parties and of men; we have found it in the Movement which we now strive to introduce to Great Britain. That pilgrimage in search of this idea has exposed me, in particular, to many charges of inconsistency. I have no apology to offer on the score of inconsistency. If anything, I am disturbed by the fact that through fourteen years of political life, and more than one change of Party, I have pursued broadly the same ideals. For what in fact does a man claim who says that he has always been consistent ? He says that he has lived a lifetime without learning anything; he claims to be a fool. In a world of changing fact and situation, a man is a fool who does not learn enough to change some of his original opinions.

The essence of Fascism is the power of adaptation to fresh facts. Above all, it is a realist creed. It has no use for immortal principles in relation to the facts of bread-and-butter; and it despises the windy rhetoric which ascribes importance to mere formula. The steel creed of an iron age, it cuts through the verbiage of illusion to the achievement of a new reality.

Chapter 1 - Creed and System

STABILITY AND PROGRESS

In the ranks of Conservatism there are many who are attracted there by the Party's tradition of loyalty, order and stability - but who are, none the less, repelled by its lethargy and stagnation. In the ranks of Labour there are many who follow the Party's humane ideals, and are attracted by its vital urge to remedy social and economic evils - but who are, none the less, repelled by its endless and inconclusive debates, its cowardice, its lack of leadership and decision.

These elements comprise the best of both Parties: and to both Fascism appeals. The two essentials of Government are stability and progress; and the tragedy of politics is that the two, essentially coincident, are organised as contradictions. Stability implies order and authority, without which nothing can be done. It is regarded as belonging to the "Right". Progress implies the urge to reform without which society cannot survive. It is regarded as belonging to the "Left". Stability is confused with reaction and a stand-pat resistance to change: progress with ill-considered changes, or with the futile and paralytic discussions so characteristic of a timorous democracy. As a result, neither of these essentials is achieved. This is a dynamic age. Stability cannot exist without progress, for it implies the recognition of changes in the world which no political system can alter. Nor can progress exist without stability, for it implies a balanced and orderly view of the changes which have taken place.

The "Right" seeks stability, but denies the power of adaptation which makes stability an active force. The "Left" seeks progress, but rejects all effective instruments and robs authority of the power to make decisions. The result of both systems of the two great organised Parties of the State is in the end the same. Stability confused with reaction and a resistance to change, together with progress confused with obstructive debate and committee irresponsibility, end alike in chaos. Both are instruments for preventing things being done, and the first requisite of the modern age is that things should be done.

THE FARCE OF 1931

The final caricature of our present system may be found in the events of 1931. The country, wearied by five years of parliamentary stagnation, had rebelled from the Conservative slogan of "Safety First", and installed a Labour Government in office. For eighteen months, progress, such as it was, came under the aegis of dissentient committees and the dictation of discordant interests. As time passed, the Government fell under the spell of trade depression which it had done little to create, but which it was powerless to remedy. In the absence of any constructive policy, the Government came to the conclusion that it was necessary to reduce unemployment benefit, but was too weak to do this without elaborate publicity. The country - most of all, the unemployed had to be frightened: and the May committee soon produced a report fit to alarm the nation. The economics called for were duly realised, even though the achievement demanded a regrouping of political complexions. The Labour Government might have successfully purchased a little respite at the expense of its supporters, had it not been that foreign financiers had read the May report and taken it in deadly earnest. The report had been circulated to secure public approval for action which was "necessary to save the pound". But it exposed our weakness, and thus started the stream of foreign withdrawals from our banks which, in spite of £130 millions of money borrowed in support, forced us off the Gold Standard in September. A Government with a constructive policy would have averted the whole situation; a Government with authority would have reformed without apology: had even this been done, it is more than possible that the crisis might have been avoided.

We are faced today with the results of government by indecision, compromise and blether. Both political Parties, and the remnants of Liberalism as well, stand bound by the great vested interests of "Right" and "Left" which created them. In

Opposition, there is the same profusion of promise; in office, the same apathy and inertia. In post-War England, their creeds have become platitudes; they consistently fail to grapple with the problems of the time. Their rule has led, with tragic inevitability, to the present chaos. Therefore our Fascist Movement seeks on the one hand Stability, which envisages order and authority as a basis of all solid achievement; we seek, on the other hand, Progress, which can be achieved only by the executive instrument that order, authority and decision alone can give.

PARLIAMENT

It is customary to describe Fascism as Dictatorship, a term which leads to some confusion of thought. Fascism is not Dictatorship in the old sense of that word, which implies Government against the will of the people. Fascism is Dictatorship in the modern sense of the word, which implies Government armed by the people with power to solve problems which the people are determined to overcome. Modern Dictatorship implements the will of the people to action which cannot be implemented without the power of action being entrusted to Government. In this sense we accept the word Dictatorship but we do not accept it in the sense implied by our opponents. By Dictatorship we mean Leadership; by Dictatorship they mean tyranny. Fascism is Leadership of the people with their willing consent along the path of action which they have long desired. Leadership is a term which cannot be misrepresented or misunderstood and for that reason we prefer to use it.

An exceptional amount of nonsense is talked about the term "Dictatorship". We are solemnly assured that the Government of Mussolini is a Dictatorship against the will of the Italian people, but when he appeared before them in his tour of the country during the tenth anniversary of his Government he was accorded probably the greatest popular reception ever given to an individual in the history of the world. Equally fatuous is the suggestion that Hitler frogmarched forty million Germans to the Poll to vote for him, but by a slight oversight omitted the three millions who retained and exercised perfect liberty to vote against him. The plain fact is that modern Dictatorship is Leadership resting on the enthusiastic acceptance of the people and could not endure without their support. It is true that measures have been adopted in these countries more rigorous than we hope will be necessary here. The reason was that these nations had drifted so far towards collapse and anarchy before Fascism came to power.

The rigour of Fascist Government is in very exact proportion to the degree of chaos which precedes it. For that reason we appeal to Britain to return Fascism to power before the situation has so far deteriorated. Britain is great enough to adopt Fascism because it wants it before it has to adopt it by reason of national collapse. But whatever measures a Fascist Government employs must depend on the enthusiastic acceptance of the people and must emanate from their demand for action. Fascism is not a creed of Governmental tyranny. But it is definitely a creed of effective government in strong contradistinction to the present decadence of the Parliamentary system. Parliament is, or should be, the mouthpiece of the will of the people; but, as things stand at present, its time is mainly taken up with matters of which the nation neither knows nor cares. It is absurd to suppose that anybody is the better for interminable discussion of the host of minor measures which the Departments and local interests bring before Parliament to the exclusion of major issues. Such matters, in which the public interest is small, take up far too much Parliamentary time. The discussion, too, is usually futile; most of the Bills before Parliament demand technical knowledge; but they are discussed, voted on, and their fate decided, by men and women chosen for their assiduity in opening local charity bazaars, or for their lung power at street corners. This is by no means an over-statement; when a young man asks his Party Executive for a constituency, they do not ask "will he be a good member?", but "will he be a good candidate?"

In a practical system of government our political philosophy comes to these conclusions. Whatever movement or party be entrusted with Government must be given absolute power to act. The people will retain through the machinery described in the next chapter a direct control over Government. On the other hand, the power of obstruction, the interminable debate of small points within the present Party system which today frustrate the nation's will to action, must be abolished. The present Parliamentary system is not the expression, but the negation, of the people's will. Government must have power to legislate by order to carry out the will of the majority without the organised obstruction of minorities who at present use Parliamentary procedure to frustrate the will of the nation. We must eliminate the solemn humbug of six hundred men and women indulging in detailed debate of every technical measure, handled by a non-technical assembly in a vastly technical age. Thus only shall we clear the way to real fulfilment of the Nation's desire, which is to get things done in modern conditions.

LIBERTY

When we propose an effective system of Government we are, of course, charged with the negation of liberty by those who have erected liberty into the negation of action. Liberty, by the definition of the old Parliamentarians becomes the last entrenchment of obstruction.

We hear so much glib talk of liberty, and so little understanding of its meaning. Surely nobody can imagine that the British, as a race, are free. The essence of liberty is freedom to enjoy some of the fruits of life, a reasonable standard of life, a decent house, good wages, reasonable hours of leisure after hours of work short enough not to leave a man exhausted, unmolested private happiness with wife, children and friends and, finally, the hope of material success to set the seal on private ambition: these are the realities of liberty to the ordinary man. How many possess this liberty today? How can the mass possess such freedom in a period of economic chaos? Many unemployed, the remainder living in the shadow of unemployment, low wages, long hours of exhausting labour, bad houses, shrinking social amenities, the uncertainty of industrial collapse and universal confusion; these are the lot of the average man today. What humbug, then, to talk of liberty! The beginning of liberty is the end of economic chaos. Yet how can economic chaos be overcome without the power to act?

By our very insistence upon liberty, and the jealous rules with which we guard it, we have reached a point at which it has ceased to be liberty at all. We must preserve the nation's right to decide how, and by whom, it shall be governed; we must provide safeguards to ensure that the powers of government are not abused. But that is far from necessitating that every act of government must be subject to detailed and obstructive debate, and that in an assembly with little experience or knowledge of administrative problems. This fantastic system, begun in good faith as the origin of freedom, has ended by binding the citizen in a host of petty restrictions, and tying the hands of each successive government. Even in debate, the orators of Parliament no longer hope to convert one another, as they did in the days of Sheridan. The Party Whips are in attendance; a member who disobeys will soon find himself cut off from the Party - which, incidentally, paid the expenses of his election - and his chances of keeping his seat will be of the smallest. The only useful purpose of debate is to advertise each member in his constituency.

It is quite obvious that this system creates bad government and hampers the individual citizen. Constitutional freedom must be preserved; but that freedom is expressed in the people's power to elect Parliament and Government and thus to choose the form and leadership which it desires. Beyond this it cannot go. In complicated affairs of this kind, somebody must be trusted, or nothing will ever be done.

This is the kernel of our Parliamentary proposals. To some it may seem to imply the suppression of liberty, but we prefer to believe that it will mean the suppression of chaos.

ORGANISATION OF THE MODERN MOVEMENT

The same principles which are essential to Government apply, with even greater force, to a political movement of modern and Fascist structure. Here we are dealing, not with the mass, but with the men who believed in the cause, and are devoting their energy to its aims. We have seen the political parties of the old democracy collapse into futility through the sterility of committee Government and the cowardice and irresponsibility of their leadership. Voluntary discipline is the essence of the Modern movement. Leadership in Fascism may be an individual or a team, but undoubtedly single Leadership in practice proves the more effective instrument. The Leader must be prepared to shoulder absolute responsibility for decision and must be surrounded by a team equally prepared to take responsibility for the functions clearly allocated to them. For the only effective instrument of revolutionary change is absolute authority. We are organised, therefore, as a disciplined army, not as a bewildered mob with every member bellowing orders. Fascist leadership must lead, and its discipline must be respected. By these principles, both in the structure of our own movement and in the suggested structure of Government, we preserve the essentials of the popular will and combine them with the power of rapid decision without which the nation will ultimately be lost in chaos. No man need join a Fascist movement and accept its leadership who does not wish to do so and the subsequent Fascist Government will be submitted to a direct vote of the people as a whole.

The immediate task is the firm establishment of the Modern movement in the life of the British nation. Ultimately, nations are saved from chaos, not by Parliaments, however elected; not by Civil Servants, however instructed: but by the steady will of an organised movement to victory. A whole people may be raised for a time to the enthusiasm of a great and decisive effort, as they were in the election of the National Government. That enthusiasm and effort may be sustained for a long period, as it was in the war by the external pressure of a foreign threat to our existence. History, however, provides few cases in which the enthusiasm and unity of a whole people have been so sustained through a long struggle to emerge from disintegration and collapse.

For such purpose is needed the grip of an organised and disciplined movement, grasping and permeating every aspect of national life. In every town and village, in every institution of daily life, the will of the organised and determined minority must be struggling for sustained effort. In moments of difficulty, dissolution and despair it must be the hard core round which the weak and the dismayed may rally. The modern movement, in struggle and in victory must be ineradicably interwoven with the life of the nation. No ordinary party of the past, resting on organisations of old women, tea fights and committees, can survive in such a struggle. Our hope is centred in vital and determined youth, dedicated to the resurrection of a nation's greatness and shrinking from no effort and from no sacrifice to secure that mighty end. We need the sublime enthusiasm of a nation, and the devoted energies of its servants.

Chapter 2 - The Corporate State

RATIONALISATION OF GOVERNMENT

THE main object of a modern and Fascist movement is to establish the Corporate State. In our belief, it is the greatest constructive conception yet devised by the mind of man. It is almost unknown in Britain; yet it is, by nature, better adapted to the British temperament than to that of any other nation. In psychology it is based on team-work; in organisation it is the rationalised State. We have rationalised industry and most other aspects of life, but we have not rationalised the State. Yet the former makes the other the more needful, lest the economic power of man should pass beyond the power of his control.

Sir Arthur Salter has said that "private society has developed no machinery which enables industry as a whole to contribute to the formation of a general economic policy, and secure its application when adopted". It is this machinery of central direction which the Corporate State is designed to supply - and that, not as a sporadic effort in time of crisis, but as a continuous part of the machinery of government. It is essentially adaptable; no rigid system can hope to survive in a world of quickly changing conditions. It envisages as its name implies, a nation organised as the human body. Every part fulfils its function as a member of the whole, performing its separate task, and yet, by performing it, contributing to the welfare of the whole. The whole body is generally directed by the central driving brain of government without which no body and system of society can operate.

This does not mean control from Whitehall, or constant interference by Government with the business of industry. But it does mean that Government, or rather the Corporate system, will lay down the limits within which individuals and interests may operate. Those limits are the welfare of the nation - not, when all is said, a very unreasonable criterion. Within these limits all activity is encouraged; individual enterprise, and the making of profit, are not only permitted, but encouraged so long as that enterprise enriches rather than damages by its activity the nation as a whole.

But so soon as anybody, whether an individual or an organised interest, steps outside those limits, so that his activity becomes sectional and anti-social, the mechanism of the Corporate system descends upon him. This implies that every interest, whether "Right" or "Left" industrial, financial, trade union or banking system, is subordinated to the welfare of the community as a whole and to the over-riding authority of the organised State. No State within the State can be admitted. "All within the State; none outside the State; none against the State".

THE PRODUCER AS THE BASIS OF THE STATE

The producer, whether by hand or brain or capital, will be the basis of the nation. The forces which assist him in his work of rebuilding the nation will be encouraged; the forces which thwart and destroy productive enterprise will be met with the force of national authority. The incalculable powers of finance will be harnessed in the service of national production. They will not be fettered in their daily work; but they will be guided into the channels which serve the nation's ends.

This is the true function of finance, intended, as Sir Basil Blackett has insisted, to be "the handmaid of industry". There will be no room, in our financial organisation, for the unorganised operations which have led to such enormous complexities and have rocked the structure of British industry to its foundations. In our labour organisation there will be no place for the trade union leader who, from sectional or political motives, impeded the development of a vital service. But there will be an honoured place for the financial organisation which joins in the world of British reconstruction, and for Trade Unions which co-operate with such reconstruction, in the interests of members who are also members of the national community.

Class war will be eliminated by permanent machinery of government for reconciling the clash of class interests in an equitable distribution of the proceeds of industry. Wage questions will not be left to the dog-fight of class war, but will be settled by the impartial arbitration of State machinery; existing organisations such as Trade Unions and employers' federations will be woven into the fabric of the Corporate State, and will there find with official standing not a lesser but a greater sphere of activity. Instead of being the general staff of opposing armies, they will be joint directors of national enterprise under the general guidance of corporative government.

The task of such industrial organisations will certainly not be confined merely to the settlement of questions of wages and of hours. They will be called upon to assist, by regular consultation, in the general economic policy of the nation. The syndicates of employers' and workers' organisations in particular industries will be dovetailed into the corporations covering larger and interlocking spheres of industry. These corporations in their turn will be represented in a national corporation or council of industry, which will be a permanent feature in cooperating with the Government for the direction of economic policy.

The idea of a National Council was, I believe, first advanced in my speech on resignation from the Labour Government in may 1930. The idea has since been developed by Sir Arthur Salter and other writers. A body of this kind stands or falls by the effectiveness of the underlying organisation. It must not consist of casual delegates from unconnected bodies, meeting occasionally for ad hoc consultation. The machinery must be permanently functioning and interwoven with the whole industrial and commercial fabric of the nation. The machinery must not be haphazard, but systematic, and continually applied. Sir Arthur Salter envisages such machinery in the following passage: "In industry and trade, banking and finance, in the professions, there are institutions which are capable of representing more than merely sectional interests. They may have been formed primarily for defence of a common interest against an opposing organisation or against competitors of the public; but they have, or may have, another aspect; that of preserving and raising the standard of competence and the development of traditions which are in the general public interest." This latter is precisely the aspect which the corporate system develops into a smoothly-working structure of industrial government. To this end, no other concrete policy has yet been developed.

The first principle is to absorb, and use, the elements which are useful and beneficial. In this respect Fascism differs profoundly from its opponent, Communism, which pursues class warfare to the destruction of all science, skill and managerial ability; until, when it begins to feel its feet, it has to buy these same qualities at enormous cost from foreign nations. This precisely describes the course of events in Russia. The first task of Leninism was to destroy, to root up every tree in the garden - whether good or bad - merely because it had been planted by the enemy. Then, when destruction had brought chaos on the heels of famine, there came a five-year plan of American conception, implemented by a nucleus of German and American technicians hired at immense expense.

Such is not the method of Fascism, its achievement is revolution, but not destruction. Its aim is to accept and use the useful elements within the State, and so to weave them into the intricate mechanism of the Corporate system.

LOYALTY TO THE CROWN, BUT REVOLUTION IN METHODS OF
GOVERNMENT.

Whatever is good in the past we both respect and venerate. That is why, throughout the policy of the movement, we respect and venerate the crown. Here, at least, is an institution, worn smooth with the frictions of long ago; which in difficult experience has been proven effective and has averted from this Empire many a calamity. We believe that, under the same impartial dispensation, the greatest constitutional change in

British history may yet be peacefully achieved. While the position of the constitutional monarchy is unaffected and indeed is strengthened by Fascist policy the remaining instruments of government will be drastically altered by the legal and constitutional means to which we adhere, in order to provide the effective instruments of government and of action which modern problems demand.

In the first instance Fascism seeks power by the winning of a parliamentary majority at a general election. That majority will be used to confer upon government complete power of action by order. Parliament will be called together at regular intervals to review the work of the Government. In the intervals Fascist members of Parliament will be employed as executive officers in the areas whence they are returned to Parliament. By this means Fascism will overcome an anomaly which at present paralyses effective government. Many measures of government have to be implemented by local authorities which are often opposed to the government of the day and concerned only to obstruct its work. The team of government pulls one way in Whitehall and the team of local authorities pulls the other way in the various localities. The result is a deadlock familiar to all concerned with national administration, which would not be tolerated for a moment in any business concern. It is difficult to imagine the head office of a business pursuing one policy while half its branch offices pursued another. Yet this is precisely the situation which for years past has often reduced the mild efforts of successive governments to a tragic farce. Consequently Fascism would replace the present local authorities with executive officers who would be the Fascists M.P's., which the various areas had returned. The elective principle would thus be combined with executive efficiency and the will of the national majority would prevail over obstructive minorities. They would be assisted by locally elected Counsels from which would be selected executive officers to be heads of the various departments of local government. The present committee system would be swept away under which each Councillor is liable to serve on several committees as a "jack of all trades but master of none". Each departmental chief would be responsible to the local officer or Fascist M.P. who in turn would be responsible to National Government. The Fascist principle of individual responsibility and clearly allocated function would be maintained throughout and for the first time it would be possible to assess responsibility for failure and success. By these means Fascism would provide an executive instrument to implement the nation's demand for rapid action while retaining the principle of elected representation in every element of national life.

THE HOUSE OF LORDS

Together with this reform of the House of Commons and Local Government Fascism would replace the present House of Lords by a Second Chamber of specialists and men of wide general knowledge. The House of Lords is one of the unworkable anachronisms of the present system. In days gone by the Members of the Upper Chamber were in some ways exceptionally endowed with the qualities of government. Their position had secured them education and their wealth had enabled them to travel - in these, and a multitude of other ways, they had the advantage of their contemporaries. They were hereditary land owners on a large scale, in days when the ownership of land was the only serious industrial responsibility which economic circumstance had created. Thus they spoke with authority in many matters with which others were less fitted to deal; and, so long as this went on they were a fitting and indispensible branch of the law giving body.

Their position was derived from the social inequalities of the period; and there is no social factor which time has more radically changed. As individuals, the Members of the House of Lords are neither better nor worse, richer nor poorer, wiser nor more foolish, than their colleagues in the Commons. Their only function is interference without responsibility. They have become hereditary automata, whose powers successive governments have found it necessary to truncate. Originally the

House of Lords represented in some degree the main industry and interest of the Country which was agriculture. Today they have largely ceased to represent that interest and scarcely can be said to represent any other. It is therefore only natural and in keeping with British tradition and constitutional practice that they should be replaced by a Chamber which represents in a specialist sense every major interest of the modern State. The type of interest which would there be represented would be as follows:- Representatives of the Dominions, Crown Colonies, India, religious thought, the fighting services, Civil Service, education, authorities on foreign affairs and those who have rendered the State conspicuous service. In addition, of course, the National Council of Corporations composed both of Employers' and Trade Union representatives would be thoroughly represented in the reconstituted Second Chamber.

OCCUPATIONAL FRANCHISE

Such a combination of new and effective instruments in Government will enable Fascism in the lifetime of the first Fascist Parliament to carry through the immense changes in the national life requisite to the entry of the new civilisation towards which the compelling facts of the modern age impel every advanced nation. At the end of that Parliament a new election will be held on an Occupational Franchise - a steel worker will vote as a steel worker; a doctor as a doctor, a mother as a mother, within their appropriate corporation. Party warfare will come to an end in a technical and non-political Parliament which will be concerned not with the Party game of obstruction, but with the National interest of construction. Thereafter the life of the government will be dependent on a direct vote of the whole people held at regular intervals, which in any case will not exceed the lifetime of a present Parliament. In the event of a government being defeated it will be the duty of the constitutional Monarch, as at present, to send for ministers in whom he believes the nation will show confidence in a fresh vote.

The nation as a whole will, therefore, exercise a more

direct control over government than at present in that the life of government will depend on a direct vote of the people instead of upon the intrigues of a Party Parliamentary system, which usually have no relation to the issue on which parliament was elected. The people also will secure in this parliament which assists government with technical and instructed criticism a truer representation in that they will vote within their own industries and occupations for candidates whom they know well on subjects with which they are familiar. An engineer shall vote as an engineer; and thus bring into play, not an amateur knowledge of foreign and domestic politics, but a lifelong experience of the trade in which he is engaged, he will vote in common with others of similar experience, and will give the reasoned decision of a technician in his particular trade in a choice between members of that trade. Is not this a truer representation of the individual and of the complex components of the life of the modern State than prevails at present?

As things stand at present, there is nothing to prevent the electorate, supposedly all-wise, from electing a parliament composed entirely of sugar-brokers. Each might be an excellent candidate for whatever party he chose to represent. He might well be affluent, genial and docile; a firm supporter of charity bazaars, a pillar of local football elevens, a regular contributor to the party funds of his constituency. If, with all this, he kisses babies with a pretty grace, and promises reforms enough to impress the electors, he may well find himself in Parliament. If enough sugar-brokers did it, there is no reason at all why the whole of Parliament should not be sugar-brokers: but this would scarcely fit them for the task of discussing a Bill dealing with the complexities of unemployment administration in a northern industrial town. In fact, the unemployed might expect to fare rather badly.

This is an exaggeration; but the like of it, in miniature, happens at every election. Electors vote on general considerations of policy, which they cannot understand, since the facts are not fully before them. The truth is, simply, that the issues behind every political decision are far too complicated to set before the public. The result is that elections are fought in a welter of journalistic catch-words "Three acres and a Cow"; "Tax Fortunes, not Food"; "Safety First"; "Hang the Kaiser"; "The Red Letter" and "Save the Pound" as a prelude to depreciating the Pound! This is a travesty of democratic law-giving.

The original conception of the present Parliamentary system was that free and full discussion in Parliament and at elections would instruct public opinion in the great issues of the day and thus would enable a reasoned verdict to be given by the electorate. In the degeneration of that system it has become a game of very sharp practices with the sole object of replacing the set of men in Office with another set of men who obtain their places by any panic cry which may serve the purpose of the moment however dishonest or however irrelevant it may be to the real issues before the Nation.

Opposition no longer serves the purposes of reasoned criticism and analysis of the Government's policy which exposes weaknesses and elicits the verities of National problems. Modern problems are too technical by their very nature to be handled effectively by such an assembly. Debate, therefore, is no longer constructive but purely destructive and concentrated on transient issues of popular passion which tend yet further to obscure the real issues which should receive the attention of Government. New personalities emerge and Parties come to power not by virtue of their constructive gifts but by reason of their skill in the purely destructive art of discrediting the existing Government on small and jejune points which have no bearing upon reality. New men do not emerge as they will do within the technical Fascist system by the strength of a new and constructive idea. They emerge in the slapstick comedy of Parliamentary debate as adepts in the pastime of getting jobs for themselves and their Party by any means fair or foul which smart advertising and meaningless slogans may assist. Once the game is won and the jobs secured they settle down to the respectable lethargy of Office.

The danger of our present system is the fact that it brings itself too easily into contempt. Nobody, nowadays, expects election promises to be fulfilled. Governments are elected on the strength of their appeal to passion and to sentiment. Once in office they promptly resign their effective power in favour of the great interests within the State, but yet superior to the State, who exercise their power in secret. The increasingly technical nature of all problems in an economic age has made it difficult or impossible to explain the real issues to the electorate as a whole. The division between daily politics and the reality of Government has become ever greater. The technician has become ever more enchained by the passion, the prejudice and the folly of uninstructed politics.

By such a system as we advocate, the technician, who is the architect of our industrial future, is freed for his task. He is given the mandate for that task by the informed franchise of his colleagues in his own industry. A vote so cast will be the result of experience and information. Is not this in fact the rationalised State? Is not this system preferable to the solemn humbug of present elections, which assumes that the most technical problems of modern government, ranging from currency management to the evolution of a scientific protective system, can be settled by a few days' loose discussion in the turmoil of a General Election?

The ordinary man would greatly resent such treatment of the facts of his daily industry and life. If someone strolled into an engineering shop and, after five minutes' cursory examination of an intricate process which the engineer had studied all his life, proceeded to tell him how to do it, the engineer would quickly send the intruder about his business. Yet these are the methods which our present electoral system applies to that most intricate and technical of processes, the government of a civilised State.

The Rationalised State, as well as rationalised industry, has become an imperative necessity. The Corporate State provides the only known solution to the problem. Our electoral system has become a farce, worse even than in the days of bribed elections and pocket boroughs. As it is organised at present, our system of government lacks the calibre to carry us out of trade depression and set Britain again on top of the world. As time goes on, the world crisis may possibly diminish ; but even in that event we are not organised to emerge in a position comparable with our former prosperity. After the crisis of 1921 - a crisis far less severe than that of 1932 - we did not recover even the semblance of our old prosperity; government must be rationalised if we are to avoid a repetition of the last decade of unhappy history. On the other hand, if the clouds of depression do not lift, and the State remains un-rationalised, there is a very real danger that the farce will be recognised as such, and that the country will turn - and turn violently - to the catastrophic remedies of Communism.

Chapter 3 - The State and the Citizen

THE moral and social law and convention of Britain provide the most startling of all contrasts with the Briton's strange illusion that he is free. The plain fact is that the country is hag-ridden. In no other civilised country, except perhaps in the United States, has the individual so little freedom of action.

We live on public anarchy and private repression: we should have public organisation and private liberty. We are taught that it is an outrage to interfere with the individual in his public capacity as producer, financier or distributor - though, if he uses his powers badly, his anti-social conduct may damage tens of thousands of his fellow-citizens. But we are taught to interfere with every detail of his private life, in which sphere he can damage no one but himself, or at most his immediate surroundings. A man may be sent to prison for having a shilling bet on a horse-race. But he can have a tremendous bet on the stock market, and live honoured and respected as a pillar of industrial finance. He may damage the whole life of the nation in the capacity of capitalist or trade union leader, but he may not even risk the slightest damage to himself by obtaining a drink after the appointed hour!

We are treated as a nation of children; every item of social legislation is designed, not to enable the normal person to live a normal life, but to prevent the decadent from hurting himself. At every point the private liberty of the individual is invaded by busybody politicians who have grossly mismanaged their real business - which is the public life of an organised nation.

It is, of course, a simpler task for limited intelligences to keep public-houses closed than to keep factories open. The politician, conscious perhaps of his own limitations, turns naturally to a sphere with which he is more familiar. The result is the creation of a political system which is precisely the reverse of what a political system should be. In the public affairs of national life we have disorder and anarchy: in the private affairs of individual life we have interference and repression.

It is scarcely even anarchy; it is a laughable form of organised humbug, which has made us the mock of every civilised country. The whole system is the child of that same mentality which has transformed Parliament into a bleating of ineffective sheep; which blundered into the War, the Peace, the Debt-Settlement, and the Financial Crisis. It is the by-product of age, struggling with a problem for which it feels itself unequal; and, as such, it is a supreme challenge to youth and realism.

PUBLIC SERVICE - PRIVATE LIBERTY.

The Fascist principle is Liberty in private life. Obligation in public life. In his public capacity a man must behave as befits a citizen and a member of the State; his actions must conform to the interests of the State, which protects and governs him and guarantees his personal freedom. In private he may behave as he likes. Provided he does not interfere with the freedom and enjoyment of others, his conduct is a matter between himself and his own conscience.

But there is one condition. The State has no room for the drone and the decadent, who use their leisure to destroy their capacity for public usefulness. In our morality it is necessary to "live like athletes", to fit ourselves for the career of service which is the Fascist idea of citizenship. To all moral questions the acid test is first social and secondly scientific. If an action does not harm the State, or other citizens of the State, and if it leaves the doer sound in mind and body, it cannot then be morally wrong. It has been suggested that this test conflicts with religious teaching. The contrary is the case, for it coincides with every tenet of real religion. Any Fascist is free to add to this test any other moral consideration which his private conscience or religious belief dictates. Our aim is not to conflict with religion, but to indicate the Fascist conception of citizenship which is in every way compatible with religion. The Fascist is expected to live a dedicated life, but it is the dedication of manhood to a fighting cause not the dedication of a monk to withdrawal from the world and its problems.

We detest the decadence of excess as much as we despise the decadence of repression. An ordered athleticism of mind and body is the furthest aim of justly enforceable morality. And even for the enforcement of this we would rely on the new social sense, born of a modern renaissance, rather than upon legislation. The law arrests the occasional drunkard; but it does not touch the tippler, the weakling and the degenerate.

In our ordered athleticism of life we seek, in fact, a morality of the Spartan pattern. But when the Fascist State is won this must be more than tempered with the Elizabethan atmosphere of Merry England. The days before the victory of Puritan repression coincided with the highest achievements of British virility and constructive adventure. The men who carried the British flag to the furthest seas were far from hag-ridden in their private lives. The companions of their leisure hours were neither D.O.R.A. nor Mrs. Grundy.

FITNESS AND HAPPINESS

We know that happiness, no less than fitness, is a social and a political asset. The more gaiety and happiness in the ranks of those who grapple with the tasks of today, the better is it for the achievement of their mission. But all gaiety of life and happiness in private things must contribute to, and not diminish, the power to serve the State. In practice we are glad to see a man on race-course, on football stand, in theatre or in cinema during well-earned hours of leisure; and we do not mind in the least seeing him in a public-house or club, provided that he is not there to squander his health or his resources. In many things the distinction is between relaxation and indulgence. The latter becomes decadence, but the former contributes to healthy enjoyment, which in its turn contributes to efficiency and to service.

Therefore, in asking our members to "live like athletes" we do not advocate the sterility of Puritanism and repression. We want men in every sense of the word in our ranks, but men with a singleness of purpose which they order their lives to serve. We expect our members to keep fit, not only in mind, but also in body, and for that reason we have often been attacked as organising for physical violence. We shall certainly meet force with force; but this is not the motive of these activities. No man can be far sunk in degeneration so long as he excels, or even performs competently, in some branch of athletics. It is a part of the dedicated life of a new movement to maintain that constant training in mind and body which is readiness to serve when the time comes. In our own movement, in fact, we seek to create in advance a microcosm of a national manhood reborn.

Such is our morality, which we claim is the natural morality of British manhood; and from it follows hostility to the social repression and legislation of today, and to every achievement of our hag-ridden politics which is summarised in D.O.R.A. We seek to create a nationwide movement which will replace the legislation of old women by the social sense and the will to serve of young men. Every man shall be a member of the State, giving his public life to the State; but claiming in return his private life and liberty from the State, and enjoying it within the Corporate purpose of the State.

WOMEN'S WORK

Our organisation began as a men's movement because we had too much regard for women to expose them to the genialities of broken bottles and razor-blades with which our Communist and some of our Socialist opponents conducted the argument until the Blackshirt movement was strong enough to overcome these tactics. Now women play a very important part in our organisation and will be increasingly valuable in our work as we develop our electoral organisation. The part of women in our organisation is very important but different in some respects from that of the men; we want men who are men and women who are women.

In the political organisation of the Corporate State we envisage a highly important part for women. Professional women and those engaged in industry would, of course, find their natural representation in the corporations which cover their industry and their profession. The greater question remains of the representation and organisation of the great majority of women who seek the important career of motherhood, and who have never yet been represented as such in any organisation.

To many the idea may seem fantastic, but the logic of the situation seems to demand some Corporate organisation and representation of motherhood. It is a truism to say that motherhood is one of the highest callings, and of the utmost importance to the State; why, therefore, should women not be accorded representation and organisation as mothers? Normal women have hitherto suffered greatly from the absence of representative organisation. Their representation has drifted into the hands of professional women politicians, irreverently described as the "Members for No Man's Land. Such women are perhaps adequately qualified to represent certain aspects of women's life, but few of them have any claim to represent the mothers of the nation. Why should not the representation of motherhood be an organised force in the counsels of the State? The care of mother and child is an integral part of the Fascist State, which regards itself, not only as the custodian of the present, but also, in far greater degree than the Old Parties, as the custodian of the future.

There are many questions which are of primary interest to women, and which an organisation of this kind would go far to solve. Questions of housing, health and education in their widest application, come naturally within its sphere And there remains matters of still wider political and social significance - on which the counsels of womanhood must be of first importance.

The great majority of women do not seek, and have no time for, a career of politics. Their interests are consequently neglected, and their nominal representation is accorded to women whose one idea is to escape from the normal sphere of women and to translate themselves into men. That process in the end is never very effective, and the attempt makes such women even less qualified than the average man to deal with the questions of home and of children.

Consequently, the representation and organisation for the first time of normal women, on whom the future of the race depends, are a practical political necessity. Fascism, in fact, would treat the wife and mother as one of the main pillars of the State, and would rely upon her for the organisation and development of one of the most important aspects of national life.

Chapter 4 : The Foundations of Policy

(1) THE WORLD'S OUTPUT

BEFORE proceeding to examine the detailed economic machinery of the Corporate State, it is first necessary to discuss the economic analysis which leads us to the conclusion that the present order of industry, and consequently of society, must be replaced by the economic policy in which we formulate our constructive alternative.

It is the common form of old gang economics to assume that the present crisis is a temporary phenomenon which, in the end, will pass away automatically without any particular effort of man or any drastic reorganisation of society. One of the leading exponents of that view once argued with me on the following lines: - "You are a young man who cannot remember previous depressions; they have often occurred before in my lifetime, and have passed away. All these things to which you refer, such as the rationalisation of industry and the displacement of man's labour by machinery, have been going on for long past. They were met in the past century by a gradual rising of wages which increased the power to consume, and by a gradual shortening of hours which reduced the power to produce. Above all, in due time fresh markets opened overseas to absorb our surplus production. For instance, when I was a boy, Negroes did not ride bicycles; now they do ride bicycles, and workers are employed in Coventry to make those bicycles".

It was useless to point out to him that these crises of over-production in relation to effective demand had usually been temporarily overcome by such fortuitous events as the discovery of the Rand Goldfield, which led to a world inflationary movement. Although at the time he was in charge of the nation's finances, our protagonist of the old economics had but slight acquaintance with monetary problems.

Apart, however, from these complexities, the real and simple answer to the "negro-and-bicycle" school of thought can be briefly stated. It is true that during the course of the last century greater production was roughly adjusted to demand by the automatic processes just described, albeit with great suffering to the working class, and with struggle and dislocation of the industrial machine. It is true, also, that we managed largely to dispose of our surplus production by the sale of manufactured goods to countries not yet industrialised. Repayment of that surplus sale could of course never be made, without dislocation of British industry, by the acceptance of goods or services in return to an amount equivalent to the surplus which we had thus alienated. Payment consequently took the form of foreign investments from which the bond-holder drew a small annual tribute in the form of interest, and on the manipulation of which the world-wide financial strength of the City of London was largely founded. Foreign investment, through the medium of such sales abroad of our surplus production, became one of the chief aims of British financial policy, and was largely the origin of the great school of Liberal-Labour thought which holds that the sole criterion of British prosperity is the amount of goods which we can send abroad for foreigners to consume.

Be this as it may, the system worked at least sufficiently well to prevent a collapse of industry and of society. But our "negro-and-bicycle" statesmanship, in surveying with complacency its past experience, ignores certain new factors of the modern age. In the first place, during the course of the last generation the scientific advance has been more sudden and disconcerting than ever before in history. As a great scientist once put it to me, "During the course of the last twenty years science has advanced more than it did in the previous two hundred years, and the only minds not to register that change are those of the senior politicians". In other words, science, invention, technique have recently increased the power to produce out of the range of all previous experience. In the meantime, our machinery of distribution and of government has remained practically unchanged, with the result that the production of industry greatly outstrips effective demand. In the second place, the foreign markets of countries not yet industrialised are daily ceasing to be available. Our previous markets are themselves being industrialised, and are sheltering their nascent industries behind prohibitive barriers.

These two simple facts - (1) the new scientific advance; and (2) the artificial closing of our former markets - provide a sufficient answer to the "negro and-bicycle" theory without research into complexities such as monetary theory hitherto regarded as outside the sphere of statesmanship. On that side, only this need be said for the present. If any fortuitous event occurred today, such as the chance discovery of goldfields which temporarily saved the economic system in the past, the effect of that happy accident would be rendered negatory by the deliberate policy of certain great countries in sterilising gold. It is true that a powerful movement now exists for monetary reform, and few things are more comical in the face of modern politics than the spectacle of politicians solemnly drawing the attention of Parliament to the existence of a monetary problem who previously denied its existence with all the indignation of outraged orthodoxy.

While we welcome this belated conversion, we nevertheless suggest that monetary reform, unaccompanied by far deeper measures of national rationalisation, is in itself entirely inadequate to meet the present situation. I myself have a consistent public record, extending over the last decade, of struggle for monetary reform against the combined effort of Old Gang politicians and bankers to resist it. Nevertheless I believe that the importance of monetary reform (vital as it is) is today out of proper perspective. Let us assume that all the policies which our older statesmen have resisted too long and studied too late were actually applied. Let us assume that the world price-level was stabilised, in agreement with other nations, by the international regulation of gold, or even by the agreed management of currencies. Let us assume that the limpid intelligence of the present Prime Minister, in conference with Mr. Roosevelt resolved the world's monetary problem, and that the substitution of that happy word "reflation" for "inflation" makes the process at last respectable. Let us also, if you will, assume that reparations and inter-allied debts were wiped out by clear-cut decision of an international conference, and further, that national tariffs were universally reduced to a minimum.

Even if we make the immense assumption that all the problems which are now so much canvassed as barriers to trade were surmounted by the statesmen who are now discussing them, we should still have to overcome certain bedrock facts for which the existing political system and existing statesmanship offer no solution whatsoever. We should still be faced by the fact that the industries of the world can today produce, without running at nearly their full pressure, far more than any conceivable effective demand of the present system can absorb. That is the central fact which neither talk nor conference has yet escaped, and which, indeed, has not yet been seriously considered by statesmanship.

This proposition will today scarcely be disputed on the evidence available, but in all discussions of the unemployed problem it is almost always ignored. It is ignored because it involves a fundamental change in the machinery of the government and of industry. So the ostrich brigade of Old Gang politicians and economists plunge their heads yet deeper in the sands of important but minor problems which should have been tackled years ago, but the solution of which would bring us now but little nearer to world stability.

The above figures show, in a simple form, the significance of the modern movement towards rationalisation. The process has been applied in every field of production. In every case the result has been the same - products at first cheapened and employment stimulated, while the new market was tapped and satisfied;

then, as the large profits of the pioneers attracted more tardy adventurers, an excess of capacity to produce over the power to consume. There comes a point, in all commercial expansion, where the output of bicycles increases faster than the ingenuity of those who seek negroes to sit upon them.

The process of rationalisation, advanced as it is, has still far to go. Broadly speaking, it is furthest advanced in the United States. Twenty American families working on the land, Mr. Hubert Blake has estimated, can produce the food needed for themselves and eighty other families; in France, it takes fifty families to produce the food needed for themselves and fifty others.

The process of competition, national and international, forces a tendency towards more and more rationalisation. However much wheat there may be, the tendency of the future will be for French cultivators to struggle towards greater output per head, rather than for American cultivators to do the reverse. In industry, as well as in agriculture, the movement is the same. In the case of boots and shoes, where there are a multitude of separate processes and where rationalisation is therefore more difficult, the Czechoslovakian workman, in the highly mechanised factories of the late Herr Bata, produces twice as many boots per day as does the workman in British boot factories. The movement of the future will be towards a higher world average per workman, and thus to increasing rationalisation in Britain.

It has been calculated by Mr. Fred Henderson that in the United States, sixty-seven men can produce the goods which 100 men were needed to produce before the war. A third of America's workmen would, therefore, be permanently idle - without even sporadic employment - had not a higher standard of living contributed towards absorbing the surplus. This is a world-wide tendency; and it is vital for Britain, as for other countries, that living standards should be raised so that the greater output should be consumed.

One of Britain's chief industrial difficulties has been the lack of fluidity of output. Our productive energies flow in established channels; neither labour nor capital willingly seeks for new forms of enterprise. This has been the result of our childish faith in the huge markets for our export industries, in our capacity to recapture markets in which our goods were no longer wanted. We can produce more bicycles than we can find negroes who wish to ride them; and a multitude of countries, which used to buy from us, are making their bicycles (and other things) themselves.

Even in 1929, at the height of the industrial boom, the world was far from consuming as much as it could produce. There were a million unemployed in Britain, whose output nobody would buy. The American steel industry, admittedly running on optimistic estimates of consumers' needs, was never working at its real capacity. There was already a surplus of the staple crops. Among primary raw materials, copper and zinc outputs were already restricted; rubber was grotesquely in excess; and tin, with supplies accumulating in warehouse, had new schemes of expansion, and vast mechanical installations, becoming productive month by month.

In face of this evidence, it is quite clear that the power to produce has far outstripped the mechanism of distribution. The relatively slow increase in productive capacity during the last century gave time for the automatic adjustment of demand to supply; this has now given place to a sensational advance in science, technique and productive potentiality, which makes irrelevant all hope of the automatic adjustments of the past.

Only by a new structure of governmental organisation can we hope to meet the consequences of industrial organisation. Nothing but the rationalised State can hope to overcome the problem created by rationalised industry. It is idle to denounce rationalisation, because it simply means the modernisation of industry, and industries which are not modernised cannot live at all in present conditions. Further, to prevent rationalisation is to prevent any reaping of the fruits of science which, in any rationalised society would vastly benefit mankind. The way to meet industrial rationalisation is not to put back the hands of the clock, but so to organise society that its effects are constructive rather than destructive. That organisation is described in a later chapter, but to arrive at that solution we must first face the situation created in the present system by rationalisation.

It cannot be denied that every day new processes of rationalisation displace fresh labour. The displacement of labour creates more unemployment, reduces the number of those earning wages, and thus yet further reduces the market for which industry produces. The power to produce goods increases, but the power to consume goods does not increase - at least in anything like the same proportion. If the power to consume increased in anything like equal ratio to the power to produce, the labour displaced by rationalisation would of course be absorbed in industry again, by the greater demand for goods. As no machinery of government or of industry exists to secure this end, the labour thus displaced is not re-absorbed. The effect of rationalisation, in fact, is not to increase, but rather to diminish, purchasing power by the increase in unemployment. Yet we need at the present time an increase in purchasing power, not only sufficient to provide a market which can absorb the labour at present unemployed, but also adequate to create new labour for those whom the future processes of rationalisation will throw into unemployment.

This is the problem of under-consumption which remains when all the temporary dislocation and disturbances, on which the attention of politicians is now exclusively concentrated, have been resolved. It is a problem which makes irrelevant all calculations based upon the trade-cycle theory of the past. We are so often told that the present world depression is all part of a recurring trade cycle which moves continually from boom to slump and back again. The protagonists of the trade-cycle theory argued in the same way in 1921, and they were wrong. Britain revived, certainly; but throughout eight years of recovery she never regained her old position, or absorbed her unemployed into productive industry.

This consideration appears to be even more valid in the present "recovery". The usual Stock Exchange "boom "has been accompanied by an even slower process in absorbing the unemployed into industry. The facts of the present situation justify up to the hilt the Fascist theory that booms of the present system will tend to get shorter and slighter in effect while depressions tend to get longer and more severe. Within the system, boom and depression will alternate as before but underlying all these transient phenomena is the crisis of the system which arises from the factors set out in this chapter.

We are faced with a crisis of present civilisation partly world-wide and partly peculiar to ourselves. So far, Great Britain is one of the few great countries which has made no serious effort to meet its permanent implications.

(II) BRITAIN'S PARTICULAR PROBLEMS

We have so far examined only those considerations of industrial crisis which apply to the world as a whole, and which account, at least in part, for the world crisis. It is necessary, however, also to consider the peculiar difficulties of the British position, which, even if these world factors were absent, would involve a fundamental revision of our industrial organisation.

It must never be forgotten that Britain is the greatest exporting nation, dependent more than any other country on the markets of the world. We were the first nation to pass through an industrial revolution, and for long we enjoyed something approaching a monopoly of the world trade in manufactured goods. Long before the War, that monopoly had passed away, and under the stress of war and post-war development the process has been progressive and accelerated. Nevertheless, our export of manufactured goods still amounts to nearly 30 per cent, of our total production. In relation to the new and special difficulties of our position, the first fact to note is the rapid industrialisation of our former markets.

INDUSTRIALISED MARKETS

In the great Free Trade theory of the last century, which, like other beautiful dreams, has broken under the hard test of actual experience, all nations were to produce the products which they were fitted by nature to produce, and to exchange them with the corresponding products of other nations.

In actual fact, each nation is striving hard to make itself as nearly as possible a self-contained economic unit. Behind every kind of artificial barrier, they seek to create a variety of trades to supply them with as large a proportion as possible of the goods which they consume. No matter whether the goods thus produced cost their consumers more than if they were purchased from us ; no matter if the processes of the new industries, be economic or uneconomic; we have to face the fact that nearly every civilised nation is striving to produce at home an ever greater quantity of the goods which it consumes. Further, the backward and undeveloped areas of the world, which we previously supplied with manufactures for their consumption and with capital goods for their development, have mostly reached a point of development in which they need such services in ever lessening degree. The capital goods have borne fruit. We sold them, for example, textile machinery; now they both spin and weave, and Lancashire has lost its markets. We have to face a situation very awkward for the nation most dependent on foreign trade - that our foreign markets are inevitably shrinking.

Nowhere, unfortunately, has this tendency been greater than in the countries of the Empire. Between 1914 and 1924, the Balfour Committee calculated the rates of duty on British goods in South Africa increased on the average by 20 per cent. In other

Dominions and parts of the Empire, however, the increase was still more remarkable; in Australia, the rates increased by 56 per cent. In India they increased by nearly 300 per cent.

A typical example of the tendency may be found in Australia, and more especially in the treatment of woollen manufactures. In 1922 the Commonwealth Bureau of Commerce and Industry stated that the tariff was intended "to admit goods of British origin on the most favourable terms possible consistent with the development of load manufacture."The High Commissioner, in a pamphlet issued in London, stated officially that "if the present rates do not provide duties sufficient to protect new industries, consideration will be given to providing sufficient protection on the first revision of the tariff after the establishment of new industries".

Australia produces raw wool in great bulk and, for the most part, of fine quality. In the past, most of this has been sent to Yorkshire, where the climate has proved extraordinarily favourable to the spinning and weaving industries. To spin worsteds in Australia is, and always will be, far more expensive than in the West Riding. Australia was undeterred by this. In their textile mills, at great expense, they manufacturer damp atmosphere; and they are content with a low output from highly paid operatives working in an unhealthy moisture to which they are unaccustomed. In spite of these handicaps, a press and pamphlet campaign successfully urged the establishment of spinning, weaving and the manufacture of hosiery, blankets and other woollen products. The avowed object was, to quote once more from the Bureau of Commerce and Industry, "that Australia shall manufacture eventually practically the whole of her wool clip into woollen and worsted goods".

The result was inevitable. The following figures show our exports of wool manufactures to Australia in 1913 and 1933:-

	1913	1933
Woollen and Worsted Yarns (lbs)	1,705,000	107,400
Woollen Tissues (sq yds)	9,668,000	711,200
Worsted Tissues (sq yds)	6,223,100	235,100

In Bradford there are workers unemployed; while at the Antipodes, Australians are expensively dressed in cloth of uncertain quality.

This is a glaring example, but it is typical of much which has been happening in almost every country. Our former markets are being rapidly industrialised, and are making for themselves goods which we formerly supplied. Brazil, awake to her vulnerability as a producer of little else but coffee, has developed the textile trade, the manufacturer of boots and shoes, and a number of other trades with a total output valued at about £45 million a year. Argentina has more than doubled her industrial production. Chile has replaced with home produce much of her former imports; in cement, for example, more than three-quarters of her imports have been dispensed with. In the East, too, the same tendency has been at work. Just before the War, India, China, Japan and Australia were producing steel at the rate of 360,000 tons a year; this output has since been nearly trebled.

This is no passing phenomenon. "The general tendency towards the growth of local manufacture", wrote the Balfour Committee, . . . "is based on the inevitable desire of progressive countries to achieve some degree of diversification in their industries". Therefore, they infer, "it is impossible to expect that the general tendency will be reversed, or slow down".

In other words, much of our export market is lost for good. It is no longer merely a question of regaining it by lowering our own costs of production. These markets are closed against us by artificial barriers, no matter what the cost of our production or how low the price of our goods. It is the fixed determination of foreign nations today to build industries of their own, and to exclude our products. To this end they are not only employing tariffs of ever-increasing severity: they are rationing, and even forbidding, imports; and they are obstructing purchases of foreign currency, so that goods, once imported, cannot be paid for. Some nations restrict imports from each country to the amount which those countries buy from them. In other countries there are licences, quotas and embargoes, to say nothing of a veto on dealings in foreign exchange.

These countries have fostered, within their own borders, small local industries which, at a price, can and do satisfy local needs. These industries, having been artificially created, depend on continued support. The Governments concerned cannot, in all fairness, break faith with their own people and remove a protection upon which big money risks have been taken, and by which substantial employment has been afforded.

Thus we are no longer contending with surmountable tariffs. We are dealing with trade barriers which, though they may change in form, are permanent in effect. Our goods are not discouraged and taxed: they are definitely and designedly excluded. Yet we are frequently told that the only way out of our troubles is to lower our cost of production in order to recapture our foreign trade. Two ways are suggested to that end: (1) rationalisation, the effect of which on our unemployment problem has already been discussed; (2) the reduction of wages, which means the progressive reduction of the power of our own people to buy goods, and consequently the progressive reduction of the home market.

In fact, we are invited to drop the solid reality of the home market which we hold in our own hand, under our own control, in order to grasp an illusory export trade which must elude us, for the simple reason that foreign markets are now closed against us, whatever our cost of production.

The dilemma of our export trade in relation to necessary imports, together with the whole complex of trade balance, will be dealt with in another chapter. It is only necessary, for the purpose of the present analysis, to point out that the hope of solving our unemployment problem by an expansion of our export trade, which has long dominated the Old Gang mind, is one of the most grotesque of their illusions.

Apart, even, from the exclusion of our goods from foreign markets, the extent of that illusion may be judged by figures from official sources which I gave in a House of Commons speech on my resignation in may, 1930, which were never challenged in debate and which apply with even more force to subsequent developments. I examined first the hope of reducing the unemployment problem by an expansion of export trade to be achieved by lower costs of production consequent upon the rationalisation of industry. In four big groups of rationalised trades between 1924 and 1929 an average increase of 20 per cent, in production was achieved, but at the same time an average decline of 4 per cent was shown during this period in the number of workers employed. If by corresponding measures of rationalisation we had increased our export trade by £200 million per annum (which was necessary to make good the then shrinkage of our export trade), with a corresponding result on the employment afforded by the trades effecting that expansion, the net reduction in the number of those employed in these industries would have amounted to 5 per cent. If, on the other hand, we had achieved such an increase in our export trade merely by participating in a natural expansion of world trade over a period of four years without any new methods of rationalisation or displacement of labour in the industries involved, we should have put 900,000 people in employment during a period in which the normal increase in the working population was one million; thus, at the end of the period, we should be back where we began.

It was not necessary to say much more in disproof of the easy belief that the unemployment problem in Great Britain could be solved by an expansion of export trade, whether achieved by the rationalisation of our industries or by a natural increase in world markets. Even such calculations, however, are now rendered irrelevant by the simple fact - which I anticipated in the same speech - that our export trade cannot be greatly expanded, and will probably shrink yet further, because our foreign markets are being rapidly closed by artificial but insuperable barriers erected against us by nations determined to foster their own industries.

NEW COMPETITORS

In addition to all this industrialisation of former markets, we have to face, in whatever markets remain, an intensity of competition without precedent in previous experience. Many of these competitors, too, are nearer than we to the markets for the goods concerned, and better fitted to appreciate the problems of manufacture and sale arising from geographical and racial differences. America in relation to our South American market, and Japan in relation to our Eastern markets, possess geographical and other advantages so obvious that they need not be stressed. In addition, a country like America, which hitherto has disposed of only some 8 per cent, of her surplus production in export trade, has a clear advantage in a price-cutting scramble for markets over a country such as Britain, which has diverted a 30 per cent, margin of her total production to export trade.

A country, like a business, may dispose for a time of a small proportion of its total output at a loss, in order to invade further markets and to crush competitors. There is another point. Protected industries, such as those of the United States, provided that they have a substantial market at home, can charge prices which allow them to pay overhead charges and the interest on all their capital by selling the bulk - but not the whole - of their output. It then pays them to sell the rest, for export, at prices which pay merely for the labour and materials used. A business, or a nation, can do this with 8 or 10 per cent, of its output; but

Britain, in order to compete would have to adopt the same policy with 30 per cent, - in many industries more - of her industrial production. To attempt such a course is the direct road to bankruptcy. It would involve either the extinction of profits, or thus the slow death of commercial enterprise; or else the drastic reduction of wages, which, by diminishing purchasing power at home, would finally extinguish the one market on which industrialists can rely.

The effect of the geographical advantages of other countries may be seen in our trading position with the United States. Before the War, we supplied 16 per cent., of the goods imported to the United States, and were some way ahead of Germany, our nearest competitor. Now, though the total trade is much larger (in a normal year), our share in it has fallen to a little over 10 per cent., and we have lost first place in the trade to Canada, whose share has risen from 7 to 11 per cent. In the meantime, the United States, themselves highly industrialised, are exporting their surplus in competition with our main production. A smaller proportion of their total is actually sold in Great Britain, though the amount bulks large in relation to British trade. But in Canada, and in South America, spheres of influence are being established, and American manufacturers have rapidly gained ground against our own. In Argentina, the British share of the import trade has fallen from 31 to 24 per cent., while the United States share has increased from 14.5 to 21 per cent. In Brazil there is the same tendency; though Britain's share is slightly increased, that of the United States has risen from 16 to 22 per cent. In Canada, too, the same tendency has been more than ever noticeable.

What is true in the Western hemisphere is true also in the Eastern. Cotton yarns and manufactures have for long been one of the mainstays of the British export trade: even in 1931, they accounted for £56.6 millions, or nearly a fifth of the manufactures which we sell abroad. But we have lost our yarn export trade to Japan; and Japan, finding increasing competition from India and China, has turned her serious attention to piece goods. Since the

War, the number of cotton spindles in the Far East has increased by 80 per cent., the number of power-looms having also risen by 40 per cent.

We are faced, in fact, with a new and intensive competition for foreign markets. The intensity of the struggle for foreign markets is further increased by the shrinkage of all home markets, which drives the industrialists of every nation ever more desperately to see a foreign outlet for their surplus production. The shrinkage of home markets is, of course, in turn aggravated by the race in wage reduction, in order to lower costs and capture foreign markets, which sets up a vicious circle of shrinking home markets and greater pressure to sell abroad.

It is now the declared aim of every great nation to have a favourable balance of trade. Every nation, in fact, seeks to sell more to others than it buys from them - an achievement which, it is clear, all nations cannot simultaneously attain. So a dogfight for foreign markets ensues in which the weaker nations go under, and their collapse in turn reacts upon the victors in the struggle by a further shrinkage of world markets. A continuation of the present world struggle for export markets is clearly the road to world suicide, as well as a deadly threat to the traditional basis of British trade.

These phenomena appear at first sight to support Marxian theory. "In the decline of capitalism, all nations must strive increasingly to dump abroad their production which is surplus to the power of home consumption. A world scramble for markets ensues, with competitive industrial rivalries which lead inevitably to collapse and to war. Marxists overlook the fact that certain natural tendencies, and even natural laws, can be and have been circumvented by the will and wit of man. The law of gravity, for example, has been flouted by the aeroplane: the Marxist law that, under capitalism, all wages would be reduced to a subsistence level, has been set aside by a variety of artificial means. In just the same way, it is fair to suppose, a well governed nation can avoid the disasters incidental to the world's present industrial over-capacity.

What has been done by accident and of a rough and crude method for a period, can be done permanently under scientific planning. But those tendencies will not be defeated by letting things alone; and it is here that Conservatism falls down. Some of the Marxist laws do actually operate if mankind is not organised to defeat them, and they are operating today in the inchoate society which they envisage. If we rely on the instruments of the Stone Age, we shall be subject to the laws of the Stone Age and overwhelmed by its forces. In other words, if we rely on Conservatism to defeat Marxism, we shall be defeated by Marxism.

SCIENCE AND MASS PRODUCTION

Underlying all these phenomena is a deeper sociological fact, which destroys for all time the illusion that our old time supremecy can be regain in the old way. In the past, British goods gained their ascendancy, partly because they were first in the field, but also because they were the best.

Mass production has altered the criteria; the skill of the hand craftsman is no longer the leading factor in industry, and buyers are increasingly influenced by the price. Here we are at many disadvantages. In the past, export has been our main problem, and we cannot afford to sell goods abroad except at a full economic price. In each market we are apt to encounter some near-by competition who is simply getting rid of his surplus at any price which will pay him to keep his mass-production machinery running. Again, most of our workmen are of a good type, capable of rising to the heights of skill which earned them their reputation in the past. For modern, cheap mass production, such labour is unnecessary. No limits are now set to the exploitation of the backward labour of the Orient in competition with the skilled labour of the West. An Oriental can work for ten hours a day in exchange for a few bowls of rice, provided that such labour does not exact too much from his fragile physique or from his undeveloped intelligence. To press a button at regular intervals in the simplified processes of mass production while he dreams of other things, is to him most appropriate and congenial labour. He is actually, in some ways, better suited for the monotony of mass-production tasks than is white labour, which often cannot endure that monotony, at any rate for more than very short hours. The development of Oriental labour for mass-production purposes is only in its early stages. That tendency is bound to increase and to become a deadly menace to the whole white standard of life, and indeed to the whole structure of Western civilisation.

In addition, even in our own market, scientific methods of mass production raise very serious problems. In the period 1925-29 the world's population was increasing by 1 per cent, each year, but the output of crude products was growing at the rate of 2.6 per cent. In manufacturing industry the rate of increase was obviously faster still, the main incentive, to quote the League of Nations report, The Course and Phases of World Economic Depression - coming "from an extraordinary advance in industrial technique - rationalisation in agriculture as well as in the manufacturing industries." The output of a man-hour or a man-day has increased to a colossal extent, both here and abroad. If it had occurred merely in this country, the displaced labour might have been absorbed in an expansion, through cheapness and commercial enterprise, in the export trade. But, in view of the problems outlined above, it is clear that such a course was impossible.

SELF-IMPOSED HANDICAPS - THE BANKING POLICY

So far only natural barriers to British trade, which have latterly arisen or remarkably increased, have been examined. In addition to natural handicaps, however, we have subjected ourselves to self-imposed burdens unequalled in the history of any other nation.

In the post-war period, almost every industrial country (except the United States) devaluated its currency. This meant that old debts, fixed in terms of money, became very small in relation to the goods which that sum of money would buy. Most industrial companies had debenture-debts, which they were able to pay off at absurdly little effort to themselves. And governments also redeemed all their redeemable internal debts.

The result of this course of events was that foreign nations emerged from their crises with a lightened burden of taxation and with industries unencumbered with prior charges. This, in effect, amounted to a reduction in costs. In Britain, however, the reverse was happening. Most nations, by a crude inflation, escaped the burden of national debt, debenture charges upon industry and other fixed interest-bearing charges and burdens; we chose to pursue a policy of acute deflation. The result of that policy was roughly to halve the price level and consequently to double the real burden of the National Debt since 1920, and correspondingly increase the burden of every deadweight charge on industry. In addition, by the policy of artificially raising the exchange value of the selling price of our goods in foreign currencies was continually raised, and the selling price of foreign goods in our currency was continually lowered. Conservative, Liberal and Socialist Governments alike went one better than traditional Free Trade by erecting artificial barriers against British exports and giving artificial bonuses to foreign imports.

The effect was a constant disequilibrium of British prices with the rest of the world, and consequently a constant demand for lower production costs in the shape of lower wages, which led directly to a series of devastating industrial struggles. Every employer had to sell his finished product in a world of lower prices than that in which he had purchased his raw material and labour costs. This induced, not only industrial losses and bankruptcies, but also a reluctance to manufacture for stock which, by making it impossible for British manufacturers to make quick delivery, resulted in the loss of business. Every worker was faced with a demand for lower wages to be enforced by the lash of widespread unemployment created by the artificial restriction of credit in pursuit of a deflationary policy. The only classes to benefit were the rentier class and the big finance houses with large overseas interests. The rentier class benefited because, by the halving of the price level, the fixed number of pounds per annum which they were paid in interest on their gilt-edged securities were made to buy double what they had bought before. The big finance houses were assisted by the financial prestige in the international money market accorded by the portentous fact that Britain had returned to the Gold Standard at pre-war parity. To serve them, the producer, whether employer or worker, received blow after blow; the whole industrial fabric of Britain was rocked to its foundation.

That policy came to an inevitable and ignoble failure in August 1931, when the formation of a National Government combining all the men who, in their several Parties, had been most responsible for that policy, failed to preserve the artificially supported £ from collapse.

They failed despite the borrowing of a large sum. of money abroad intended to support the exchange, and used in fact in a losing gamble for which the taxpayer had to foot the bill. The only effective purpose of that borrowing was to hold up the £ long enough for foreign interests to transfer their money abroad. The same statesmen who previously borrowed to support the £ have recently borrowed another £150 million (Exchange Equalisation Fund) to keep low the £ which their Government was formed to keep high. In the circumstances, the latter transaction was right; but what a confession of imbecility it presents, in the light of their previous efforts to maintain our exchange far above its natural level!

At the same time that our older statesmen were pursuing this policy in national finance their intimate friends and trusted colleagues in the great finance houses were borrowing short from

America and lending long to Europe on highly profitable terms. Instead of bending the energies of British finance to the sadly-needed re-equipment of British industry, they were very busy re-equipping against us our industrial competitors in the rest of the world. They were caught in this profit-snatching process by the collapse of large areas of Europe in world depression.

Their loss was the nation's loss in the shock to our financial structure. Throughout this period, all who suggested the intervention of Government, either for the assistance of British industry in re-equipment or for the provision of useful and economic work of national importance for the unemployed, were dismissed as financial lunatics. Loans might be raised in London to give work in the Argentine or Timbuktu, to enrich those countries and to provide work for their inhabitants ; but we were told that loans raised in London to enrich Britain and to provide work for our own people would jeopardise our whole financial structure.

One of the main factors in my long struggle within the late Government, which led to my resignation, arose on this very point. Ministers and the City were so busy helping every country except their own, with the results that are now so familiar, that anyone who dared to raise the forgotten flag of British interests became a pariah in our political system.

Can we then be surprised at the present condition of Britain, when to all our natural handicaps in the new world was added this additional burden by Governments who acted with the customary subservience of all political Parties to the alien power within the State?

CONVERSION

The series of conversion operations has been hailed as the excuse for, and the triumph of, our financial policy. On this subject only this need be said. Broadly, conversion may be achieved in two ways -

(1) Through the inherent strength of a nation's industrial and financial position, when the Government's credit will stand high and will be reinforced by a proportion of current profits seeking a safe, gilt-edged, investment.

(2) conversion may also be secured by the simple process of making all industrial investment so unprofitable that the investor is driven to gilt-edged securities. If investment is concentrated on gilt-edged stock, the Government may profit by the competition for such securities to reduce the rate of interest. In fact our financial policy made industrial investment unprofitable by a remorseless deflation, which greatly benefited the bond-holder. By this latter method the conversion operations have been achieved. Conversion was made possible by discrediting British industry, rather than by making the Government's credit sound. Throughout a period of conversion, when the English market was supported on a 3.5 per cent, basis, British Government stocks were available in New York at prices showing a yield of over 5 per cent. Some millions per annum have been saved to the Exchequer at the expense of one small class of bond-holders. The remaining holders of Government Stock and of all gilt-edged securities, have enjoyed, by reason of these operations, an appreciation of their capital amounting to hundreds of millions, and the dead-weight charge on industry and the Nation has been correspondingly increased. Conversion, in fact, has been secured by the methods of deflation and of credit restriction, which have resulted in enormous industrial losses.

Chapter 5 - The Old Gang's Answer

IF our trade position had been really sound when we suspended the Gold Standard we should have experienced a considerable trade boom and reduction in unemployment figures. Such was the experience of nearly every other country in the first effect of currency depreciation. For that reason the suspension of Gold, which our Government had spent £130 million to avoid, was hailed as the good news for which industry was waiting. Since then we have participated in no very marked degree in a partial world revival in which our position was greatly assisted by the artificial and temporary expedient of currency depreciation. The consequent slight decline in our unemployment figures was gathered to the credit of our rulers despite their strenuous efforts to prevent the currency depreciation to which it was almost entirely due. In particular we are informed that Britain's position is relatively more favourable than that of other countries although other great nations have achieved a greater percentage reduction in unemployment figures without the assistance of currency depreciation.

Such arguments are little more than a drug; the reasoning is not only deceptive, but dangerous, as it lulls the nation again into false security and dulls the sense of action and of effort.

In fact the most alarming feature of the present situation is that unemployment figures have not sensibly decreased in our present position of abnormal and temporary advantage to British industry occasioned by a 30 per cent, depreciation in our exchange without any corresponding rise in our internal price level. The effect of this situation is that we enjoy a large bounty upon our export trade, and that we are sheltered from foreign imports by an effective exchange barrier to which we have recently added a protective tariff. We shall enjoy these advantages so long as our price-level does not rise in proportion to the depreciated exchange. At present we still enjoy them, but our unemployment problem is unaffected.

In other countries, where the exchange has been depreciated, there have invariably been industrial booms until the price-level was readjusted. British experience has been unique. We had no boom before the slump; we have had no boom after the currency was devalued. This phenomenon indicates in fact, a deeper-rooted industrial malady than the most pessimistic have yet diagnosed. It may well be that in the present depression of world prices our internal price-level may show no sign of rising in proportion to exchange depreciation for a longer period than the usual time lag; and even when a rise in internal prices does occur, it will probably be not nearly equivalent to the exchange depreciation. By our failure to maintain the £ and by other temporary factors in general price tendencies, we have, in fact, achieved by accident the position of a low exchange rate without an increase in the internal price-level.

In these circumstances it is effrontery to claim that our position is improved. The only shred of advantage lies in the fact that our goods in the few countries where they are welcomed, are cheaper to the foreign buyer; and that, at home, foreign goods have become more expensive. Our vast unemployment, our reduced industrial profits, our mania for economy in productive public works, and our general loss of spending power - all traceable, directly or indirectly, to the deflationary policy of successive Government - have gravely detracted from the advantages which might have arisen from the exclusion, for currency reasons, of foreign goods. In the export markets, restriction has increased and multiplied; there is scarcely a country where the British industrialist can be sure of getting his goods in, or of receiving payment after he has done so.

The advantage, such as it is, is temporary and fortuitous. At any moment one of our great competitors may suffer currency depreciation, and our momentary advantage will be wiped out. In nearly every country controversy concentrates on the possibility of inflation and of currency depreciation, and one or more of these countries may at any time re-enter that phase. So far, therefore, from regarding our relatively favourable unemployment figures as a reason for taking things easily, we should regard this accidental respite as a breathing space in which to reorganise our industries and strengthen our commercial defences.

No greater disservice to national interest can be performed at the present time than the twisting of facts which in reality are unfavourable, to the service of the dope machine. The Old Gangs have not only reduced industry by their policy to its present plight; by their soporific propaganda, with its artificial sunshine of " relative improvement", they have deceived the public and have paralysed the national will to action.

THE POLITICAL SYSTEM

In the more permanent field of political reconstruction, the leaders of the old parties have nothing to offer. Theoretical Socialists saw the solution of their fancy in a Socialist commonwealth, where production is for need and not for profit, where every law of present economics is set aside. They describe their goal with a certain precision: but none of them, so far, has even attempted seriously to describe the road by which they reach it, or how they will bridge the interval between the collapse of all present machinery, consequent on the adoption of Socialist measures which are incompatible with it, and the establishment of the alternative machinery of State and of industry which they envisage. They tell us, in fact, that we live in hell, and that the heaven of Socialism would be a better place ; but by an oversight they omit to tell us how to get from one to the other.

The old position of evolutionary Socialists such as the Webbs, which was relatively logical, has long been rendered irrelevant and untenable by modern conditions. In their thesis, society would evolve peacefully and gradually to Socialism. Industries would be nationalised one at a time by cautious experiments; no fresh step would be taken until the last was confirmed. So, by gradual stages of natural evolution and development, mankind would arrive at the Socialist Commonwealth with universal acclamation, as the reward of his experimental successes.

This thesis assumes a static society during the course of the evolutionary experiment; such an assumption has been roughly confounded by the hard facts of a dynamic age. Collapse and universal disintegration now threaten unless action, and universal action, is taken. In an age of urgent change, we have no time for evolutionary process. If Palaeolithic man were brought to life today, he would be killed by the traffic long before he had time to evolve into a modern homo sapien. He would have to think of something quicker than evolution. The Socialists of the old school are in much the same position as Palaeolithic man. They can only advance by evolution, and the age they live in has no time for that. Before they had socialised half a dozen industries, the fabric of society would have succumbed to the depression. Their theories, therefore, are by now of no more than academic interest.

The Independent Labour Party, on the other hand, seeks "Socialism in our time" by methods which would entail the scrapping of all existing machinery. In the period of transition, there could be nothing but the most thorough anarchy: and thus they would precipitate the collapse and the struggle which their benevolent pacifism seeks to avoid. Their living-wage policy seeks to secure a vastly higher standard of life in this country than prevails elsewhere, without any protective measures to prevent the under-cutting of that standard by cheaper foreign labour; presumably this will persist until the sweet light of reason has invaded the darkest recesses of Africa, and every Hottentot has been persuaded to join the I.L.P.

Whatever germ of sense may be latent in these proposals is destroyed by clinging to the Free Trade fetishes of an obsolete Liberalism with which the I.L.P. is riddled. But apart from this Liberal obsession, the proposals of the I.L.P., in brief but not unfair summary, become an attempt to transform society by measures which would immediately precipitate its collapse, in the roseate belief that the lions of the great vested interests will learn in our time, by peaceful persuasion, to bleat the Internationale in happy harmony with the lambs of the I.L.P.

The more realistic Communist, on the other hand, does not shrink, in theory at any rate, from the consequences which his proposals involve. He points to his Communist goal and frankly informs us that he is prepared to wade to it through the blood of class war by the overthrow of existing society. True that in a developed and highly technical society such as Britain, largely dependent on foreign supplies and the interactions of world trade, something like half the population might starve or be destroyed in a protracted civil war before the Communist purpose was achieved. These minor considerations do not deflect the Communist from his steady purpose to achieve a solution which he believes to be the only escape for humanity. The position is at any rate clearer-headed and more honest than the performances of the theoretical Socialists of Labour and the I.L.P., who gallop up to the fence of class struggle and then stop short of the logical conclusion, leaving the nation to fall into the Communist ditch.

These posturing Girondins with the heads of Communists and the chicken hearts of Social Democrats have no place in the realities of the modern age. No more than Socialist and Communist can stand-pat Conservative or Liberal provide a solution. The stop-gap measures of unscientific tariffs, borrowed from the programmes of the last century, allow the same chaos to operate behind the protective barrier that operated before.

A later chapter will show why Protection, unsupported by National Planning and the rationalisation of the State, takes us no further than before, as our experience of National Government begins to prove. There is only one alternative to our present steady drift to collapse and the anarchy of Communism: that alternative is the ordered political economy of the Corporate

State. The economic machinery of that State will be described in the next chapter. For the moment it is only necessary to note in our economic analysis that the dilemma of rationalisation, of science and of modern technique applied to industry, adding to unemployment and national distress, remains unanswered by any political party, and that failure to answer that dilemma must lead in the end to collapse.

It may be that small boom periods of ever shorter duration and of ever more hectic character may precede that collapse. When for a time demand is almost at a standstill, monetary stimulants and similar measures may temporarily increase demand in order to satisfy the elementary needs of the world.

The ineluctable fact remains that the power of modern machinery and production can so rapidly satisfy any demand of that character that saturation and clogging must soon again ensue. Each fresh seizure of that nature is likely to be more severe as the pressure of the modern machine increases, until at last its power of output leads to something approaching universal apoplexy.

This analysis is simply the facing of facts. This is the pre-requisite for action, and the gloom of the outlook must not be taken as a signal for despair. Had facts been faced before, we should long ago have had a policy of constructive action. No nation of such virility, and so great a tradition of achievement, would have allowed things to drift so far if its mind and its will had not been paralysed by the opiate propaganda of bewildered politicians, who steadily refuse to face facts which they and their system are not strong enough to overcome. Like children in the dark, they put their heads under the bed-clothes rather than get up like men and grapple with the danger.

Chapter 6 - Building up the Home Market

IF our economic analysis has any validity, we must found any constructive policy on the basic fact that present consuming power is inadequate to absorb the production of modern industry. Consequently, the economic solution is not the reduction of our standard of life, but the raising of that standard to a point at which the increased purchasing power of the home market can absorb the increased production of modern machinery. How to raise wages, salaries and the standard of life to that point, without the dislocation of industry which such a process would involve under the present system, is the problem to which the Corporate machinery alone provides an answer.

That the power of consumption is inadequate to absorb production is at present scarcely denied in any quarter; yet every policy of the moment seeks yet further to reduce that consuming power by the reduction of salaries and of wages, and by an all-round decrease in the standard of life. Our doctors all diagnose the malady as a lack of markets, which are simply the power of the people to buy goods; yet the treatment which all prescribe by a reduction of the standard of life, is a further inoculation of the germ which has caused the disease. It must at once be admitted that in the absence of Corporate organisation, much truth exists in their argument. An industrialist may know that, by cutting the wages of his workers in common with other industrialists, he is merely reducing the purchasing power of the market for which his industry produces. But the industrialist also knows that, if he does not reduce wages, he himself will be undercut and driven out of business, in an unregulated competitive system, by rivals who do reduce wages.

A Government may know that by reducing the wages of its employees and by reducing its service to the community, it is merely further reducing the market, the poverty of which has created the serious industrial situation which is reflected in declining revenue returns. But the Government also knows that in a period of declining revenue it must reduce expenditure or be faced by Budget deficits; the latter may, indeed, be temporarily supported, but, if indefinitely continued, they will lead to financial collapse.

So industry and Government alike are forced to measures which yet further reduce the market, and yet further aggravate the industrial evils from which both are suffering. Each fresh reduction of purchasing power deteriorates the situation, yet every instrument of national life in the grip of the present chaos is compelled to pursue that policy. At last the Government and the nation are reduced to the absurd and impotent position of a dog chasing its own tail in whirling circles of accelerating futility and disaster. How to break that circle is the major question of the age, and to it the Corporate system alone provides the answer. We have to establish a machinery of Government and industry in which it is possible, not only to maintain, but to raise, the standard of life without dislocation of industry and of Government.

Italian Fascism, in early and tentative experiments in the Corporate system, has often intervened effectively to prevent wages being reduced. It has so far failed to provide a system by which purchasing power is provided at all adequate to absorb the power of modern production. Such a task, of course, is exceedingly difficult of achievement in a country of small natural resources and little tradition of organisation; it involves at least a measure of temporary "insulation" from world economy as a whole. That task in that country has not yet been really attempted, and its comprehensive conception has scarcely yet been considered. Italian Fascism has succeeded in preserving the economic situation of Italy in a world situation in which without Fascism, it would undoubtedly have collapsed; it has also succeeded in raising the standards of the working-class in these adverse conditions; but in a small country it has not proved possible to advance in the Corporate system towards the policy which will now be discussed, and indeed such conceptions go far beyond anything which Italy has yet worked out.

It is by no means an easy task to absorb, within the purchasing power of the home market, the swollen output of modern manufacturing machinery. It is even more difficult to relate this achievement, which may have dangerous effects on production costs in its initial stages, to the necessity for carrying on an external trade to pay for our essential imports of food and raw materials.

Viewed in the aggregate, it is a task entirely beyond the scope of present-day statesmanship - not for lack of personal capacity, but because there is not the necessary machinery. In a Parliament of obstruction, discordant committees, talk and inertia, the problem is insoluble. Nothing but strong executive government can bring it to a successful conclusion.

THE NEED FOR SCIENTIFIC PROTECTION.

The first essential of a stable and enlarged home market is, of course, a scientific protective system. It is impossible to have stability without some immunity from the chaos of world conditions and fluctuations described in the previous chapter; and it is impossible here to raise wages and salaries to the point where increased purchasing power will absorb modern production in the home market, unless those wages and salaries are protected from cheap foreign competition. It is impossible to maintain, let alone to raise, the present standard of life if that standard is subject to the under-cutting of lower-paid foreign labour and to the subsidised dumping of the great foreign combinations. It is inconceivable that the home market and the economic life of these islands can be reorganised if they are subject to every factor of the world chaos which was examined in a previous chapter as responsible for our present declining position in the markets of the world.

The Free Trade argument, in present circumstances, has gone almost by default, but still finds its advocates in economists and politicians who seek escape exclusively by way of international action rather than by national organisation. Two fallacies are involved in these Old Gang economics, one of practice and the other of theory. In practice, it is demonstrably an illusion to believe that all nations can be persuaded to act effectively together. Innumerable conferences on tariff barriers, monetary problems and international co-operation have been held for the past decade, with the practical result that the barriers became greater and the co-operation less. Our politicians have attended conferences at Geneva and ad hoc conferences at every other Continental watering-place, cap in hand as supplicants to the rest of the world to be reasonable in order that Britain may live.

In hard and bitter experience, their policy simply has not worked. Other nations, by very crude and old-fashioned methods, have merely tried to protect themselves in the general sauve qui peut of Europe. The international policy implies by its very nature that more powerful and intelligent nations must wait on the advance of the less intelligent and enlightened. The march of every nation is reduced to the pace of the slowest. We have to wait until the gentle charm of Socialist and Liberal persuasion has penetrated the darkest corners of the earth before we can begin to maintain, let alone to advance, the British standard of life.

Surely the time has come to save ourselves by scientific measures of protection at a time when lesser nations are busy trying to save themselves by unscientific measures? Practice is a greater force than precept in the modern world. The first nation which sets its house in order, and discovers a modern and scientific form of industrial organisation, will lead more rapidly to a world order of economic sanity than all the resounding appeals to our common humanity which have echoed in a variety of languages through the halls of Geneva and Lausanne.

Let us now examine the fallacy in theory of the remaining adherents of the Free Trade school, who seek salvation in international action at Geneva, Lausanne and elsewhere rather than in taking off of national organisation. Their theory is derived from the period of poverty economics. In the past century we were faced with the problem of poverty; in this century we are faced with the problem of plenty. Then the question was how to eke out the meagre resources of mankind; now the question is how to release for consumption the vast resources with which science has endowed mankind. In the period of poverty any barrier to the thin trickle of international trade was obviously bad; in the nineteenth century the Manchester school of Free Traders had much reason on their side. Barriers to international trade, goods produced in countries unsuited to their production, were all factors liable to result in distress and starvation in a world community whose resources barely satisfied the needs of life.

But today we have entered the period of potential plenty, and these factors are largely irrelevant. Today, in organising production, we have to think, not so much of maximum output, as of maximum consumption. Modern industry and science can produce more than enough to satisfy the needs of man, provided that political organisation enables the machine to work. The advance of science has been the decisive factor in the change from poverty economics to the economics of plenty. Let us, in the name of reality, have done with the economics of poverty.

Hitherto no solution has been found because the more incisive brains of the old school are obsessed with the idea of international action. They cannot imagine any way of escape except by international agreement. They cannot conceive a nation organised with the technique of modern science to supply the vast majority of its own requirements from its own resources. Consequently, their attention is continually diverted from the real task of national organisation to a pursuit of the international will-o'-the-wisp through the quagmire of conflicting politics and confused economics among all the more backward nations of the earth. In pursuit of that policy, meanwhile, they have exposed to all the shocks of world chaos the struggling remnants of our industry which cater for the demoralised home market.

SCIENTIFIC PROTECTION VERSUS CONSERVATIVE PROTECTION.

The Government has now been driven, by the hard pressure of fact rather than by any process of reason, to the adoption of a half-baked Protectionist system. Without further thought, or consideration of modern conditions, it has taken over the Protectionist policy which Mr. Joseph Chamberlain first advanced some thirty years ago. Happily immune from the painful process of fresh thought, the Conservative party has advocated it ever since, and has now applied a policy which is by that margin out of date.

As a result, we have, not a scientific plan, but a rapid and inefficient improvisation. They have handed over the fiscal system of the country to a struggling committee of appointed business men who are vested with wide powers, but are endowed with inadequate information and with no machinery.

This abdication of the function of government of course imposes upon that committee a superhuman task to which it will prove inadequate. In that bottle-neck will probably be clogged the life-blood of industrial organisation. Apart altogether from the question of machinery, which we will deal with later, no vestige of scientific protective policy has yet been adopted, except very inadequately in one instance. The whole basis of modern and scientific Protection is lacking. No machinery whatever is provided for raising, or even for stabilising, the present standard of life, which is the main justification for a protective system. Protection is not made conditional upon industrial efficiency, upon good wages to the workers or upon low prices to the consumers. Our standard of life is in some degree protected from the competition of foreign employers who pay low wages; it is in no degree protected from the competition of British employers who pay low wages.

The same wage-cutting dog-fight, which means an ever-diminishing home market, may rage behind the protective barrier in the absence of any State machinery to make Protection conditional on good wages and decent conditions. Every British employer who uses Protection to raise the standard of life in his industry, and thus to contribute to an enlarged home market, may find himself under-cut by less patriotic and less scrupulous rivals.

Thus the purpose of the enlarged and stable home market, which is the sole justification for Protection, will be defeated; in fact, the same chaos will exist behind the protective barrier that previously existed outside it. One of the main objects of modern Protection is the diversification of production, the establishment of new industries catering for the home market in competition with products hitherto imported from abroad - industries employing, and adequately remunerating, potential consumers of one another's products.

Such an object necessitates a national plan of scientific Protection. In its turn that plan entails, not the appointment of yet another committee, but the establishment of a comprehensive machinery to secure its application. That plan and that machinery are wholly lacking from the policy of the Government.

OUR CONDITIONAL PROTECTION

It is submitted in our policy that Protection must be conditional upon industrial efficiency. That efficiency we define, broadly, as low prices to the consumer and good wages to the worker. All industrialists impress upon the public that, if they are given an assured home market, they can expand and rationalise their output, and thus, while paying high wages to the worker, nevertheless preserve low prices to the consumer; in other words, the rate of production rather than the rate of wages is now the main factor in the cost of production.

Those assurances should be translated into administrative facts. It is clearly necessary to do this, because no individual manufacturer, however well-intentioned, can maintain or raise wages if he is exposed to the undercutting of less scrupulous rivals. However much he is protected from wage cutting from abroad, he is still exposed to wage cutting at home. It is here that the Corporate system begins to operate. Protection should only be given in return for definite conditions as to wages and prices over the various groups of industry - conditions which will later be considered in the administrative machinery of the Corporations.

It is known and proved that modern industry, properly organised and working at full pressure, can both raise wages and reduce costs. But this cannot happen unless the manufacturer is protected from wage-cutting competitors at home as well as abroad. Hence, the necessity for Corporate organisation, which will regulate wages and prices by permanent machinery. Protection must protect organisation, and not chaos. Behind the protective barrier, the home market must be stabilised and enlarged, and the consumer must be safeguarded. These results can only be achieved within the structure of the organised system which is the Corporate State.

Protection without Corporate organisation is no bulwark against unemployment. In countries long protected, such as Germany and the United States, we have witnessed the finest result of a Protective system followed by the inevitable collapse resulting from a lack of Corporate organisation. In defiance of all Marxian laws, wages rose under capitalism to heights dizzily above the subsistence level. By happy accident, America achieved for a time the fruits of planning. Protective duties afforded comparative immunity from the competition of foreign low-paid labour. At the same time, stringent immigration laws created a shortage of labour in relation to demand, and afforded labour a strong bargaining position on the market. That strong position, even more perhaps than the enlightenment of American employers, led to a steady rise in wages, and consequently to a steadily increasing demand for goods in a home market rapidly expanding.

The whole expanding system was supported by the policy of the Federal Reserve Board, and yet further extended by the hire-purchase system which turned every trader into a banker. Even so, it is interesting to note that, even at the height of the boom, competent authorities considered that the market "was insufficient to absorb the potential production of American industry."It is a grave mistake to point to the high wage and expansionist system of America as responsible for the evils which it served for a time to stave off. The crash came because that great system was unsupported by national organisation and regulation of a Corporate character. The "philosophy of high wages" succumbed to the first serious test.

It failed chiefly because it was never a philosophy, nor yet a conscious policy. Under the pressure of credit restriction designed to check Wall Street speculation, one manufacturer after another began to curtail his wages, and competitors were compelled to follow suit. There was no industrial planning: the system was unsupported by Corporate organisation. Its success had been adventitious; it had no resources to withstand a strain. Added to this, the credit which should have been used for industrial development and the financing of reasonable consumption was devoted to the uses of Wall Street, where shares were bid up out of all relation to any conceivable real value. The Federal Reserve Board, within the limits of their system, were able only to check credit expansion in a quantitative rather than a qualitative manner. It paid speculators to borrow money at 10 per cent, in order to buy stocks yielding only 3 per cent, on the purchase price. They were willing to do this, because their experience encouraged them to hope for capital profits of, perhaps, 50 per cent. They were speculators, and their action at that time was detrimental to every serious interest. But no machinery existed for discrimination between social-and anti-social use of credit, only for a general policy of restriction. By restriction of credit, the genuine producer was hit long before the Wall Street speculator, who summoned European short-term credits to his aid.

In an effort to check the frenzy of a few irresponsible individuals, the whole great structure of American industry was shaken to foundations which did not rest on the reality of Corporate organisation. Had private enterprise been acting in accordance with a reasoned national policy, the trouble might well have been avoided. In the stress of internal competition on a sagging market, and in the absence of any State machinery for the maintenance and correlation of wages, the high wages and the hire purchase system began to crumble, and with them the whole structure of American industry. Never was more notable the absence of a coherent national plan designed to check forces inimical to the stability of the State, and to encourage the genuine forces of production and exchange in which national welfare must rest. America made a god of unregulated anarchy in private enterprise. This, she falsely believed, was the only alternative to Socialism. Both in her success and in her failure, in her dizzy prosperity and in her cataclysmic depression, there is an instructive lesson. Throughout the boom she achieved, on a basis purely temporary, what organised planning and Corporate institutions can set on a permanent footing. The very energy of American libertarianism is the best argument for Fascist institutions.

"The task is not to find a middle way, but a new way, to fashion a system in which competition and individual enterprise on the one hand, and regulation and general planning on the other, will be so adjusted that the abuses of each will be avoided and the benefits of each retained. We need to construct such a framework of law, custom, institutions and planned guidance and direction, that the thrust of individual effort and ambition can only operate to the general advantage. We may find a simile for our task in the arch of a great bridge, so designed that the stresses and strains of the separate blocks which constitute it - each pushing and thrusting against the other - support the whole structure by the interaction of their reciprocal pressure".

The words are those of Sir Arthur Salter, a foremost product of the greatest Civil Service in the world, experienced without equal in the organisation of war and of peace. The sense of those words is the finest description yet produced in general terms of the structure of the Fascist State. He has not yet reached that conclusion, but he appears to have but a short road left to travel. Possibly, like many others, he may for the present be deterred from taking it by the fact that this great structure of Corporate organisation can only rest with certainty upon the iron reality of modern political organisation.

MACHINERY OF PROTECTION

It remains to consider the administrative machinery by which scientific Protection would be secured within the Corporate system. Under the original New Party proposals for scientific Protection, self-governing areas of industry were to be constituted for this purpose under organisations called Commodity Boards.

Such Commodity Boards were to advise the Minister, with whom ultimate power must rest if the authority of Government is not to be abrogated, on the measures of Protection to be adopted. Representation on the Commodity Board was to be accorded primarily to workers and employers in the industries seeking Protection; secondarily, also, to the industries affected by the Protective system and also to the general consumers' interests. Thus within self-governing areas of industry directing scientific Protection, we should not only have representation of producers' interests, both for workers and employers, but also of users' interests and those of the final consumer.

For instance, in the case of the Protection of an industry such as steel, those who use steel as a raw material for a further stage of production are affected, and also the general public who consume the final finished article.

In a scientific Protective system all these interests must be harmonised if industrial peace and the stability of the system are to be secured, together with the interest of the nation as a whole.

Also it is necessary that the workers should be assured that they will share in the fruits of Protection in the shape of better wages and conditions; they, too, must therefore be represented on the organisation governing the Protective system. The dual objective of our Protective system, which is good wages and low prices, would thus be ensured by the representation of both workers and consumers in the Protective machinery. Scientific Protection would shelter efficient industries catering for an enlarged home market. By this system, Protection was to be lifted out of the domain of Whitehall and the haphazard functioning of ad hoc committees, into the sphere of a permanently functioning machine of industrial self-government which continually harmonised the conflicting interests of the industrial system.

These Commodity Boards, each of which was to cover appropriate areas of interlocking industries, were in turn to be represented on a National Planning Council which formed a more comprehensive industrial synthesis, and whose purpose was to plan, regulate and direct the general Protective system of the country.

Such a system was, of course, an immature adumbration, reached quite independently, of the wider structure of a complete Corporate system. The conception of Commodity Boards representing producers' and users' interests in industry, and those of the general consuming public, can be quite naturally transformed into the organs of the Corporate system. The Commodity Boards would be comprised of the employers' and workers' organisations forming the industrial Corporation, the full functions of which have been described in an earlier chapter; to these would be added representatives of consumers' interests.

The same areas of industrial self-government in matters such as wages, conditions of industry and the general direction of regional industrial government, would also logically cover the Protective system which sheltered this area of industrial organisation.

In the more developed conceptions of the Fascist Movement, consequently, the Corporations would embrace all these varieties of function and would find their national synthesis, not merely in a National Planning Council to deal with the Protective system, but in a National Corporation acting directly under a Minister of Corporations which would in practice amount to a parliament of industry.

The function of the National Corporation would be to plan, to regulate and to direct the whole national economy, under the guidance of the Minister, who himself would have to account for his work in Parliament; which, in the reconstructed system, would be largely elected on an industrial and occupational franchise.

The consequence of such organisation is not, as in Socialist organisation, to submit industry to the government of Whitehall, but rather to provide for the self-government of industry, within a series of self-governing areas or Corporations of industry, which find their national unity in the National Corporation, and their ultimate subordination and relation to the national interest as a whole.

Within the sphere of the Corporate system would fall the re-planning of our industrial organisation - from detailed questions, dealt with by the various industrial Corporations, to the general policy of national economic development handled by the National Corporation.

In the National Corporation itself would be involved and represented the major questions of banking and financial policy, and their relation to industry, which will be dealt with in a later chapter.

How otherwise can the transition from an old parliamentary system to a modernised industrial structure be undertaken? The opponents of this conception must either resort to government from Whitehall of the absolute Socialist variety, or revert to the laisser-faire of the Victorian school. It is manifestly absurd to claim that Parliament on the present model, or ad hoc committees appointed by that Parliament, can fulfil such a task. We must either establish logical areas of industrial self-government and planning, which are synthesised in a national machine for the planning of general national policy; or we must drift from crisis to crisis with the sporadic, ill-informed and tardy effort of the Cabinet and Parliamentary system to protect us.

What other escape has been suggested except the Corporate or Fascist system The words "national planning," first used by the New Party, have since been subject to many vicissitudes. They have been made hideous by every long-haired theorist who shrinks from the hazardous and arduous corollary of planning, which is action in modern political organisation. How can the scientific re-planning of national economics be reconciled with the control of an old parliamentary system the membership of which is recruited by competitive promises to produce in five minutes a new heaven on earth at the taxpayers' expense?

Future organisation is a matter for technicians, with the ring kept free for the operation of science and organisation, by the universal authority of an organised and disciplined modern movement That is the real function and purpose of the politician in the modern age. Thus can be achieved the great necessity of steadily and systematically increasing the power to consume as science and rationalisation increase the power to produce.

Thus, and thus alone, can be adjusted the infinite complexity of modern economic organisation to the difficulties of political government. He who talks of planning within the limits of the present parliamentary and political system either deludes himself, or physically shrinks from the effort and the danger of real and fundamental reorganisation.

At this stage nobody should attempt to describe every detail or a system which can only be achieved by experiment and that practical use of experience which is the essence of Fascism. But we can at least advance, in more than broad outline, a system which by scientific Protection in return for industrial efficiency (meaning good wages and low prices) can insulate this country from the present world chaos and can provide a permanently functioning machinery for the raising of standards as this may be justified by the march of science and the increase of productive capacity.

The adjustment or that insulated economy with the rest of the world on which, after every measure of internal reorganisation, we must depend to some extent for supply of certain foodstuffs and raw material, will be discussed in the next chapter.

Chapter 7 - The Export Trade

In a previous chapter I have outlined a Corporate structure of industry which, in a continually functioning system, not only adjusts the difference of interests in industry, but also provides machinery for the general planning of our economic lives and for the raising of the standard of life. By the same machinery, a flexible and scientific Protective system is devised by those engaged in industry and cognisant with its facts, subject to the continual check and safeguard of the industrial interests affected, and also of consumers' interests, so as to maintain that machine in national equilibrium.

This plan, as already explained in detail, seeks deliberately to insulate the economy of Britain from the shock of present world conditions, and to raise the standard of life in these islands far above the world level, as the only practical means now available of finding an outlet for the vast productive capacity of the modern industrial machine.

Wages, Production and Costs

We now reach, admittedly, the most difficult part of the scheme, which is the adjustment of that national economy with world economy. The intelligent critic will say, "Let us assume that you can, by your Corporate machinery, raise the standard of life and the purchasing power of the people to a point adequate to absorb the surplus production of present industrial machinery in the home market; and that you can, by your Corporate system, so regulate industrial conditions internally as to pre vent under-cutting in wages, which would lead to the collapse of that structure. Even when you have achieved this, you will still be faced by the fact that we are more dependent than any other nation on the markets of the world, and that it is always necessary for us to maintain a large export trade in order to pay for essential foodstuffs and raw materials which we cannot produce at home.

By raising wages and standards internally, you will raise the cost of production, and thus will jeopardise that export trade; while even if that were not the result of your internal measures, you still have to show how you will maintain our essential export trade in face of all the adverse factors which you have already described, and which you have stressed to a greater extent than any other political movement."

Such very legitimate and reasonable inquiry may well be raised at this point. Our first answer, in general terms, is that it is a mistake to assume that the raising of internal standards will raise the cost of production and thus will jeopardise our export trade. It has already been pointed out that the cost of production in rationalised modern industry is determined, not nearly so much by the rate of wages, as by the rate of production.

The genius of a Ford in America has already proved that it is possible to pay the highest wages in the world, and at the same time to put on the market the cheapest article in the world. The genius of a Morris at home has already travelled far in the same direction. The limitation of the Englishman was the absence of so large and so assured a home market. The real point is that, if industry is given a large and assured home market, which it can be given by the combination of scientific Protection with the organisation of a higher standard of life, it can work at full pressure, and by its great rate of production can bring down costs even if it has to pay high wages.

Anyone who has given serious attention to the facts and figures of mass-producing industry is aware that it is scarcely an exaggeration to say that granted a certain rate of production for an assured market, the rate of wages becomes almost irrelevant. Consequently, it is a proven fallacy to assume that a high rate of wages in these islands need generally raise the cost of production in our export trade. If our industries are working at full blast on the safe basis of an assured home market, they may even be able to reduce production costs in an effort to reach out for the capture of the world's markets.

In fact, the measures we have suggested for internal organisation should assist, rather than handicap, our export trade. Each industry will be exporting a surplus rather than the bulk of its production. It will be able, even should its costs be high, to meet the terms and prices of its overseas competitors. Like American industry in the past, British industry will be assisted in disposing of its export surplus, by the existence of a large home market which enables it to increase the rate of production, and consequently to lower its costs.

THE TRADE BALANCE

"But," the objector will reply, "you previously argued that foreign markets are closing against us, whatever our cost of production, by reason of the determination of foreign nations to bar our goods from their markets, which they desire to serve from industries which they are themselves creating. How do you get round the fact of local industrialisation and abnormal competition, and all the other factors which you have enumerated as undermining our position in foreign markets?"

Here we reply frankly that of course our industry must pass through a great transition from production for foreign markets to production for the home market. In our future economy it is very improbable that so large a proportion as 30 per cent, of our total manufactured products could find an outlet in world markets, nor is it necessarily desirable that they should.

We must admit that the arbitrary and artificial interference of foreign nations with the flow of trade will probably confront us in any circumstances with a dwindling volume of exports. To shirk this fact is to be unrealistic, but the facing of the fact is no occasion for despair. We have for so long been taught by the Liberal-Labour school that the chief criterion of British prosperity is the amount of goods we can send abroad for foreigners to consume, that we are disposed to accept any reduction in our export trade as a sign of ruin. This facile assumption is made without any analysis of the facts and figures, and without any inquiry whether it is possible to transfer a large measure of our production from an export to a home consumption basis, and yet to maintain sufficient exports to buy essential foodstuffs and raw materials.

Of our imports, the foodstuff and the raw material group must be regarded as necessities, subject to the considerations concerning Agricultural policy advanced in the next section. A substantial proportion of these are needed for re-export after manufacture; but the same, or greater quantities of the same, or similar, materials will subsequently be needed to keep industry running for the diversified demands of the home market. It is impossible, therefore, to make any allowance on this head; on the basis of 1930 figures, £675 millions must be set down as the approximate value of our necessary imports. On the basis of 1933 figures, the amount (but little diminished in volume) is less than £500 millions.

This, then, is the necessary bill which must be met each year to serve the needs of our population and of our manufacturing industries. The actual figure is a fluctuating one; but, as our investment income fluctuates, broadly, in the same sense as the price level of raw materials as do the payments for shipping and other services, it is fairly safe to estimate that some £250 millions of imports will still fall to be paid for out of the visible export trade.

Even in 1933, we succeeded in finding a market for £365 millions of our goods, as against £730 millions in 1929, With rationalised and planned production it seems unlikely, that we could fail in the future to find outlets for £250 millions, especially as the Empire alone took £164 millions of our exports in 1932. In fact, the statistics available point to the remarkable conclusion that we could nearly achieve a "balance of trade with our present exports to the Empire alone, provided that we excluded foreign manufactured goods from this country. If in addition we can produce even £100 millions of foodstuffs in this country which we now import from abroad we could secure our "balance of trade "within a self-contained Empire without any dependence on foreign markets for our exports. It will be seen from the next section on Agriculture that it is the aim of Fascism to produce £200 million of foodstuffs in this country which we now import from abroad and we are confident that this end can be secured.

AGRICULTURE AND AUTARCHY

It will be observed from the foregoing statistics that we are very far from being unable to pay for necessary foodstuffs and raw materials once we decide to exclude the manufactured goods from abroad, the bulk of which can perfectly well be manufactured in Britain. It is the settled policy of Fascism to build a Britain as far as possible self-contained and to exclude Foreign goods which can be produced at home. If that policy was adopted we should run little risk of an unfavourable trade balance even if we lost the whole export trade with the rest of the world, exclusive of the Empire to which we supply at present £164 million (1932 figures) of exports per annum. But the great conception of a Britain nearly self-contained and an Empire entirely self-contained can certainly be secured by the possible increase of British agricultural production. At present we produce £280 millions of foodstuffs per annum in this country and import £140 million per annum from the Dominions and £220 million per annum from

Foreign countries. Fascism, under a three years plan, would exclude Foreign foodstuffs and would develop agricultural production to take its place. Few competent judges will deny that it is possible nearly to double British agricultural production once the conditions are created in which that development can take place. Those conditions are - an assured market at an economic price. The farmer can be given an economic price; (1) by the elimination of the horde of unnecessary middlemen who intervene between the farmer and the housewife to take their toll of both: (2) By raising the purchasing power of the town population through the universal increase in wages and salaries which the Corporate system secures.

The power of Fascist Government to eliminate profiteering in food and to increase the market through the Corporate system will overcome the present problem of an "economic price" for the farmer. The assured market can only be given by excluding undercutting Foreign competition. Both Tariffs and Quotas still permit the Foreign goods to come in and consequently do not benefit the farmer or permit the industry to be stabilised. Tariffs tax the consumer and quotas enable the foreigner to charge a higher price, but neither benefit the British Farming industry whose products are displaced. The salvation of Agriculture can only be achieved by the clear-cut policy of exclusion.

Conservatism always rejects that policy because it would admittedly affect the position of the Foreign investor. Socialism rejects that policy because it cuts clean across their International conceptions and affiliations. The Conservative Party has long ceased to be a Party of the countryside and has become a Party of the City of London dominated by its great alien and International interests. The City has advanced large loans to countries like the Argentine which pays the interest on its loans by the export of Beef to Britain. If the Beef is excluded the interest is jeopardised and for this reason the inactivity of the Conservative Party is very easily understood. Fascism alone combines a policy of national reconstruction, putting foremost the interest of the British Producer, with a revolutionary challenge to the alien and international interests of High Finance to which the interest of the British Producer has been ruthlessly sacrificed by all Parties of the State.

It is necessary for us to choose between the interests of those who have invested their money abroad and the interests of those who have invested their lives and money in the land of Great

Britain. Fascism alone has no hesitation in deciding in favour of the Home Producer. We will deliberately create the conditions in which British Agriculture can increase its production by £200 million per annum, if necessary, at the expense of the Foreign investor.

The future uses of British Finance will be the equipment of British industry and not the equipment of our foreign competitors against us. Repercussions of this policy on our "balance of trade" can be judged with sufficient precision. On the one hand, we shall be saved from the necessity of importing some £200 millions of foodstuffs. On the other hand, we must expect some diminution of our income from Foreign investments, which now amount to some £50 million per annum, exclusive of income from investments within the Empire, which amount to some £105 million per annum and would be unaffected by this policy. Some of the income from Services we render to the world, exclusive of the Empire, might also be affected. But as many of these services are highly specialised, such as Insurance, etc., for which other nations are not similarly equipped, the loss under this head should not be very great. No doubt exists that we stand to gain in our "balance of trade" from such development of our Agriculture, even if it involves some diminution of other sources of income. It is clear that the "balance of trade "will be favourably affected by a £200 million reduction in our imports of foodstuffs which are replaced by Home production, even if this reorganisation results in some slight reduction in the income of approximately £100 million per annum which we derive from services to or investments in foreign countries.

The capital values of Investments in Empire and Foreign countries were £2,187 millions and £1,538 million respectively in December 1930 (Sir Robert Kindersley, "Economic Journal", June, 1933). The total income derived from Investments in Empire and Foreign countries in 1933 was £155 million (Board of Trade Journal, 22/2/1934). Figures are available with regard to the division between Empire and Foreign countries of the capital sums involved in these Investments but not of the Income derived from them. If the income from these Investments is divided in the same proportion between Empire and Foreign countries as their capital value, it would appear that we derive £91 millions from Empire Countries and £64 millions from Foreign countries. Since December 1930, when the capital values given above were computed, however, considerable default has taken place in countries outside the Empire. It is therefore fair to estimate that a larger proportion of the 1933 income of £155 million is derived from Empire investments as opposed to Foreign investments than is indicated by the capital values of 1930. In fact, it should be safe to assume that our income from investments in Foreign countries does not now exceed £50 million per annum. Even less official data is available concerning the Income derived from Services Rendered to Empire and Foreign countries respectively. The total income derived from these sources in 1933 was £105 million (Board of Trade Journal, 22/2/34). It is a conservative estimate to allocate half this income to Empire sources. In fact we should be well within the mark in giving the total income derived from Investments in and Services Rendered to Foreign countries as £100 million at the present time.

The development of Agriculture considered in conjunction with the analyses of figures given in the preceding section indicate that Great Britain herself can approach very closely to the self-contained or Autarchic ideal, while the conception of a self-contained Empire is actually within our grasp. Even without Agricultural development we can nearly balance our trade within the Empire if we exclude Foreign goods from these Islands. A real policy of Agricultural revival can make that great conception an accomplished fact.

But it will be argued that these imported foodstuffs are not paid for entirely from the interest on Foreign loans or even by Services rendered to other countries, but are partly paid for by the export of manufactured articles. To that extent it is suggested that our export trade will suffer if we do not permit the entry of Foreign foodstuffs with which Foreign countries pay for our manufactured exports. But to a far greater extent the industries affected will benefit from the increase of the Home Market consequent on the increased purchasing power of the Farming population. If Agriculture nearly doubles its production for a profitable market it will also double its purchasing, power for Farming, raw materials and manufactured goods for normal use. The net effect of this transaction is to transfer purchasing power from Foreign farmers to the British farming population. To the extent that markets close abroad markets will open at home, and this argument is strengthened by two further considerations. In the first place, the whole supply of British foodstuffs for the Home Market must be paid for by the products of British Industry, while at present Foreign foodstuffs are largely paid for by interest on Foreign loans. In the second place, British industry in supplying the new market afforded by the Farming population will not have to face the unfair foreign competitors which it has to meet in the shape or cheap Japanese goods, etc., in such markets as the Argentine. So far from British export trades, such as the cotton industry, suffering from the exclusion of foreign foodstuffs in favour of British products, they stand greatly to benefit.

The only interest which stands to lose is the alien finance of the City of London which has been the most consistent enemy of the Home Producer and the most constant threat to the stability of the nation ever since the war.

AUTARCHY

The policy at which we aim is Autarchy, or that of the self-contained Nation and Empire, which I described as "Insulation" in my speech of resignation from the Labour Government in may 1930. It is based not on the economics of poverty but on the economics of plenty. It recognises that modern nations can produce almost any goods they require with present machinery. Variations in production costs between nations in modern conditions are negligible in an age of potential plenty. The problem is no longer whether the goods can be produced at the least possible cost, but whether they can be produced at all. The confusion of our present economy prevents their production owing to the reduction of the standard of life and the diminution of the Home market consequent on the anarchy of external and internal competition. To enable goods to be produced we must plan and regulate the industrial area covered by our own race, which is capable of supplying in abundance all the goods we need.

Once we can free our economic system from the disruptive forces of world competition and can release the full power of our own potential production for a regulated Home market we can enjoy a standard of life far higher than we have known in the past without any dependence at all upon the chaos of world markets. We must first free our minds from the extraordinary illusion that international trade is necessarily more valuable than national trade and that without foreign markets it is impossible for this country to live with a high standard of life. That illusion originates from the poverty economics of the last century in which the world could only produce with difficulty sufficient for the maintenance of adequate life. Modern science has altered the whole premise of the argument by changing our industrial system from a low production to a high production system and thus confronting us with a totally different problem. Once this fact is grasped we are led inevitably to the conclusion that we can only solve our problem by finding a market for the goods we can produce and we can only find that market within an Insulated and planned system of National Autarchy.

Thus we aim deliberately at creating within the Nation and the Empire a standard of civilisation so high that it can absorb the production of modern industry. It is idle to hope that such a standard can be attained if our civilisation is exposed to every shock of world chaos ranging from subsidised dumping to cheap oriental competition in the foreign market and a wage-cutting dog-fight in the Home market. The impossibility of carrying on our highly developed industries under present conditions of world competition has been partly recognised through the logic of facts by the Old Parties since I first adumbrated the policy over four years ago and it is reflected in the piece-meal legislation of the present Government. It has been my constant submission that we should develop the "Insulated" Nation and Empire by conscious and deliberate plan rather than by hurried improvisation as industry after industry is threatened with collapse. We have it in our power to restore prosperity to the countryside and there to revive the vital breed of men on whom our past greatness has rested. We have it in our power also to build an industrial civilisation incomparably higher than has yet existed in this country within an area under the control of our own race which will be an example and an inspiration to the rest of the world. We have the Power, but Fascism alone has the Will.

EXPORT TRADE ASSISTED BY CORPORATE ORGANISATION

Trade agreements with the Empire will be assisted under "Autarchy" by the Corporate System owing to the unification of industrial buying and selling organisation. Corporate organisation will similarly assist our Export Trade to hold their own in world markets during the period of transition to Autarchy.

We have already examined the general effect of internal reconstruction on export trade; by increasing the home market, and consequently increasing the rate of production to serve that market, it would assist rather than handicap export trade in its struggle for foreign markets. Certain further advantages of a Corporate system in relation to export trade must now be examined.

The whole structure of a Corporate organisation involves a greater degree of industrial unity, and consequently facilitates the pooling of resources and the strengthening of our hands in the struggle for foreign markets; such arrangements as centralised selling organisations, which have been widely canvassed and in part adopted, even within the limits of our present inchoate system, are an obvious means of attack.

In the intensified struggle for markets, British industrialists are constantly driven to reduce overheads and to pool resources and to combine for selling arrangements in foreign markets. That tendency the Corporate machine would naturally consolidate. Further, directly areas of productive industry can begin to speak with one voice, national bargaining on their behalf becomes far more practicable and much more effective. It is then possible for the nation to use, on behalf of British export trade, the immense leverage of our foreign purchases of foodstuffs and raw materials.

The Big buyer has a great advantage as a seller if he is organised to use as a seller his power as a buyer. As we tend more and more, under the Corporate system, to unify and to consolidate both our purchases and our sales, so we can use the power of the buyer to promote the interests of the seller. We can adopt as our trade motto; "Britain buys from those who buy from Britain." The translation of that slogan into the practical machinery of the Corporate system would give us enormous power to force our manufactured products into markets which are now closed against us. Several great countries are dependent to a large degree on our purchases of their foodstuffs and raw materials. In the present condition of over-production in relation to effective demand by all the primary producing countries, they could not contemplate the transfer of these purchases elsewhere without the approach of ruin. Economically, such countries are at our mercy once we learn to use our great power as a buyer. The barbed-wire entanglements which confront British products in their entry to foreign markets can be blown away by the powerful artillery of Corporate organisation.

From the adoption of the Corporate system will grow that industrial and economic unity, both in our buying and in our selling arrangements abroad, which for the first time will make effective the bargaining strength of the greatest buying nation in the world. That strength we shall use vigorously in the markets of the world during the transition to autarchy. In every sphere emerges with ever more compelling necessity the urgency of substituting the organisation and the unity of the Corporate System for the chaos of a system which is not organised as a planned and directed economic entity.

Chapter 8 - The Empire

IN the previous chapter on the Export Trade our aim of building a self-contained or Autarchic Empire was outlined.

Here the ground is already prepared, not only by kinship, but by economic conference over a long period which the timidity of statesmanship has hitherto failed to translate into an effective and comprehensive Imperial policy. Further, national economic conditions assist trade relations between the Mother country and the Empire. Great Britain is primarily a producer of manufactured products, and the remaining countries of the Empire are still primarily producers of foodstuffs and raw materials. A natural balance of exchange exists which could and should be exploited.

It is not suggested that countries such as the Dominions will be prepared to close down their nascent industries for our benefit, but it is suggested that in the realm of future development, inter-Imperial planning can arrange, by a variety of methods, for production in the various parts of the Empire according to suitability for production. In fact, by general agreement on economic policy among the Governments concerned, the future of the Empire can proceed on some form of predetermined plan.

To this end, we believe it is of the utmost importance that the Dominions should constitute with us a permanently functioning machinery of economic consultation and planning in place of haphazard and occasional conferences. We shall invite them for this purpose to send representatives to our Second Chamber of Specialists which can advise both British and Empire Governments in the formulation of an Imperial plan. No effort should be spared to weld together by consent into a great economic entity the largest and most economically self-contained area in the world, bound together as it is by a common loyalty to the Crown.

If this can be achieved, we are indeed on the high road to

an insulated system which could be immune from the chaos of present world conditions. No matter what happened in the rest of the world, this great structure of economic and political interests could weather the storm. The more we examine the potentialities of Empire and the present tendencies of trade the more practical and imminent appears the great ideal of a self-contained or Autarchic Empire; already we have travelled far in that direction, and can approach to that conception more rapidly than most people imagine.

The examination of figures in the preceding chapter has shown how much of our export trade is already safe if we can even preserve and stabilise our Imperial trade. Some 44 per cent of our present export trade goes to Imperial markets. Those markets have been, and can be again, the most rapidly expanding in the world. In natural resources and potentialities it dwarfs even the vast power of the United States. It would be folly not to seize every opportunity to advance its development. In this case, of course, we are dealing with an area not entirely under the control of the British Government, in which the susceptibilies and preconceptions of different Governments have to be considered very carefully. We shall never seek in any way to interfere with the right of the Dominions to choose their own methods of Government and develop their own policies. That right will be as carefully preserved as the complete autonomy of other Fascist Movements in the Dominions with which we are related and which now develop rapidly throughout the Empire.

In weaving the fabric of Imperial unity, we must be prepared to employ an infinite variety and flexibility of method and approach. Before the actual stage is reached of grappling with the administrative problem, we can only declare our goal of economic unity within the Empire, and our unyielding opposition to that curious school of thought which would prefer economic alliance with any foreign country rather than with a member of our own Empire.

In general, our policy would be to transfer immediately our purchases of necessary foodstuffs and of raw materials from countries which at present afford us little or no market in return, to Empire countries which afford us a large market in return. It is clear to us in the development of a Britain and Empire policy that it is necessary to face at once, with clear cut determination the import of goods from foreign countries, such as beef from the Argentine, which represent interest payments on foreign loans rather than payment for our exports. Such goods evoke no British exports in return and benefit only the foreign investor to the detriment of British industries such as Agriculture whose products they displace. These goods would be the first object of our exclusion policy, together with the goods of foreign countries which provide no adequate market for British goods in return. Purchases from such countries would be replaced either by greater British production or by purchases from the Empire in return for a greater market for our goods.

An examination of purchases and of sales to all countries of the world would show a very considerable margin of purchase existed from countries which take in return no corresponding amount of British manufactured products. In such cases, purchases could be transferred to Empire countries with advantage at a very early stage.

In the development of Empire economic unity, the existence of a Corporate State in Great Britain would be of the greatest value. Again, the unity and solidarity of industrial organisation under the Corporate system, the natural tendency to pool and to centralise both buying and selling arrangements the ability of large regions of industrial organisation to speak with one voice would facilitate the representation of British industry by government in dealing with the Dominions. Also, if the Corporate system succeeded in Great Britain, it would undoubtedly be reproduced in the Dominions, like other of our successful institutions; and in an Empire of Corporate organisations dealing direct with each other no limits could be set on the extent or the rapidity of future development.

INDIA

The problem of India presents a record of muddle and betrayal. All the old parties are equally guilty of this surrender. We challenge them all whether they accept this "White Paper" of the White Flag or disturb the slumber of Conservative conferences with minor amendments. Fascist policy is clear cut. We have a right to stay in India and we intend to stay there. We have more than a right; we have a duty to stay there. We have a right because modern India owes everything to British rule. Irrigation, railways, schools, universities, hospitals, impartial justice, every amenity which makes modern life possible for any section of the inhabitants of India was conferred by the energy of British Government.

These achievements are denounced by a tiny majority of professional agitators as alien rule. The forefathers of those who thus denounce us descended on India in successive waves of Northern conquerors. They brought not the constructive and beneficent achievements of British rule but the atrocities and rapine of the conqueror to the original inhabitants of India whom they practically obliterated. Therefore our historic right to be in India is the same as the historic right of all our predecessors; the power of original conquest. The difference is that we have used that power for the purposes of humanity and construction and not for purposes of oppression and destruction. Thus we claim the same historic right to be in India as those "Indians" who denounce us with a difference that our right is fortified by the human spirit and constructive achievement of the modern world.

A consideration of our duty is equally clear. India is not one nation but many nations; not one community but many communities. Over 250 different languages and dialects are spoken by the peoples of that sub-continent, and few of them can understand each other unless they have learned to speak English. Internally India is rent by communal differences, which in the absence of British control lead directly to massacre and crime. Externally and even within her borders India is menaced in the north by war-like tribes only too willing to repeat the long record of Indian history by a destructive descent on the softer peoples of the Southern Sun.

Any withdrawal of British authority can only result in widespread destruction of life accompanied by unthinkable atrocities and ending in a relapse into barbarism. In such conditions the duty of Britain is as clear as her right; that duty is to remain and to govern.

Thus we challenge fundamentally the premise of all the old parties of the State which contemplates by varying stages and degrees the surrender of British authority. Under Fascism, law and order will be vigorously maintained by British Government. Authority in administration will not be diminished but increased. For that authority is necessary to solve the real problem of India, which is economic. In the past Britain's contribution to Indian development has been largely economic achievement. In recent times that work has slowed up by reason of the political struggle. The beneficent power of British Government has been largely abdicated in favour of one small class of Indians whose treatment of the Indian masses, socially and economically, in private life and in factory, compares most unfavourably with British treatment. We have failed to promote the development of Indian agriculture and village industry in place of the herding together of the Indian masses in virtual slavery in the new industrial cities, the chief object of which is to undercut Lancashire goods with cheap labour for the benefit of International Capital.

British Government has been too busy answering the lawyers' points of professional politicians to get on with the job. Economic construction in India depends absolutely on strong government. At every point it is held up by religious superstition and custom. The fertile Indian plain is cultivated by archaic wooden implements because the hereditary land system maintains as sacred the landmarks of the individual cultivator. Steam ploughs are needed to cut through the Indian plains and produce fertility, but they would also cut through a tangle of hereditary landowning interests, and produce prejudice and agitation which the present British government would not dare to face. At every turn the economic reformer is inhibited by religious custom and convention which condemn an illiterate and superstition-ridden population to direst poverty. The conquerors of the past broke the idols, looted the temples and enslaved the population. Britain will preserve inviolate and intact the sacred realities of Indian religion but will override custom and convention where it is necessary to release the people from poverty. Such reorganisation demands not weaker but stronger government. It means that government must cease to argue with lawyers and must enlist the services of economic technicians.

Here lies the real outlet for the energies of patriotic and educated Indians in constructive economic works and in overcoming by an enlightened propaganda the forbidding prejudices of their less educated countrymen. In fact the energies of India as the energies of Britain must be transferred from the political sphere of talk to the economic sphere of action. If India must look to the West in place of developing her own traditional culture, let her at least acquire not the old clothes but the new clothes of the West.

Let us end this ridiculous conspiracy of English and Indian lawyers to foist on unfortunate Indians western parliamentary institutions at the very moment that the West discard them. At the moment when every advanced nation in Europe is turning from the old parliamentary institutions in order to live and to prosper in a scientific age, our little professional talkers of both nations try to persuade all Indians who can understand their arguments to adopt a proved failure.

What a sorry end to the great record of Britain in India to sell them, as the price of our surrender, this old broken down machine, just as we discard it. That would indeed be an act of treachery for which future generations of Indians would bitterly hold us responsible. We pay the new generation of India the tribute of believing that their new minds will not so easily be deluded. We invite them to join us in building in India a corporate system as we build it in Britain. That system is far more suited to Indian history and tradition than the western parliamentary system even at its zenith. In the countryside it will rest on the Village Panchayat in an election of universal franchise in which all Indians, literate or illiterate will be represented. Thus the voice of India will not be confined as under the White Paper proposals to a tiny literate class but will include the vast masses of the Indian population. From that basis we will build successive tiers of Indian representation until the voice of India is heard in the inner councils of government.

In the towns, representation will rest on both an occupational and communal basis, and again the voice of the industrial minority of India will be heard and represented. The co-operation of all Indians capable of serving their country will be sought in the great work of economic regeneration.

With such assistance strong government can cut through the labyrinth of interests to an immense increase in the standard of life. The grip of the moneylender who holds down the peasant will be broken and agricultural banks will replace his power. Co-operative marketing will follow extended irrigation in the sale of produce increased by modern methods of production. The science of the West will be linked with the spiritual urge of the East in building an India released from the present horrors of poverty and suffering.

In no country in the world is it more urgently necessary to establish the reality of economic liberty in place of the illusion of political liberty. The strong hand must be not negative but positive. Fascism alone can release the Indian masses from the grinding slavery which they suffer today. Nothing but the will of man is necessary to raise India from the depths to the heights. In Fascism the will of man, proudly conscious of the past and facing the future with an iron determination to rise to greater heights, will bring to India a peace and a prosperity within which she may pursue with a new tranquillity, her age-old mission of the Spirit from which the West still has so much to learn.

COLONIES

The Colonies would, of course, be comprised within the scope of Empire development as a unit. Foreign goods would be excluded from them with immediate and substantial benefit to British export industries. The Colonies owe everything to Britain and it is only right that they should make in return the contribution of trade concessions in a comprehensive Imperial plan. This does not mean that the native populations of those Colonies would be exploited for our ends. On the contrary, the regulation and planning of a Corporate Empire would prevent the exploitation of these populations which at present is in process. If we do not develop the backward areas of the Empire by deliberate and systematic plan; they will be developed in the chaos of uncontrolled private enterprise. Capital other than British will often jostle for their development and exploitation, with all the dangerous possibility of exploiting backward labour which the arrival of mass-production methods has created. The chaos of unregulated exploitation of cheap labour may invade the Empire as much as other regions of the world if the development is not subject to a systematic plan.

In the interests of the native population, as well as in the interests of the white standard of life, it is essential that the Colonies should be developed on Imperial plan. Much loose sentimentalism is poured out by those who in theory would hand over the earth to backward races in political self-government, but who in practice leave them an economic prey to predatory and alien capitalism. We will certainly pursue the steady course of British Colonial practice, which seeks by every means to raise native populations to a higher standard of life; but we will not

CHAPTER 8 - THE EMPIRE

pursue the illusion that great and productive areas of the world should be kept as a close preserve for races who are unable or unwilling to develop them.

If that theory had been accepted and applied in the past, the great American continent would today be a hunting ground for nomadic tribes of Red Indians, with its vast resources untapped by science for the benefit of the world. The age of sentiment has gone too far, and is producing its own logical absurdities. The earth can and will be developed by the races fitted for that task, and chief among such races we are not afraid to number our own.

The Empire and World Peace

In the foregoing section we have envisaged the development of Empire to a point where it becomes an economic entity which is Autarchic or self-contained. Some will see in any such conception a menace to world peace. They assume that a highly-organised Empire must be jingoistic and must pursue a policy of old-fashioned and aggressive Imperialism.

In fact, we claim that the economic organisation of Empire will lead to results precisely the reverse. It is true that such highly developed organisation would place in the hands of this Empire, and in the hands of those directing its destinies, an enormous power. It is equally true that any development of science or organisation puts greater power in the hands of man, which he may use for good or bad purposes. Give a man charge of a steam roller, and you equip him with great power. He may use that power to build a road or to knock down a house. The possibility of a man being so mad as to use that power for the latter purpose does not provide a conclusive argument against the use of steam rollers.

It is true that if those controlling an economically organised British Empire, and the nations supporting them, were mad or bad enough to use that power for destructive rather than for constructive purposes, the consequences to the world and to ourselves would be very disastrous. But the possibility of the whole British race going mad is not really a reason for continuing to labour in the chaos of present organisation and economics. In fact, a British Empire powerfully organised as an economic entity would be a factor on the side of world peace and stability rather than the reverse. The first race which puts its own house in order will lead, by force of the example which is worth so much persuasion, to other nations doing the same. If all went mad, the fact that other nations followed our lead might result in the highly organised and belligerent commercial rivalries which our pacifists foresee.

On the other hand, it is fair to assume that the same spirit of reason, science and serious constructive effort which is necessary to the construction of such economic organisations would still be employed in external relations when that internal construction was complete. In that event, the existence of such great Corporate organisations throughout the world would enable for the first time the economic affairs of mankind to be subject to world rationalisation.

It would be possible to end the anarchistic struggle for markets of an unorganised capitalism, leading again, as it has often done in the past, to the entanglement of governments in the commercial rivalries of their nationals. In place of that explosive chaos, rational discussion of the world economic problems would supervene. Nations which, in their internal organisation, were largely self-contained would find it a comparatively smaller problem to settle the allocation of the relatively small remaining area of raw materials which were subject to international competition, and the comparatively small remaining area of international markets which were subject to the intensive competitive struggle for those markets.

The iron realism of Fascist government in several great countries which have struggled through, the collapse of their political systems to the construction of Corporate organisations, would hardly be likely to wreck the world in a Gadarene plunge to world war and suicide. Rather, confronted by similar organisations in political character and government, they would settle down together in a practical and business-like way to solve whatever problems still led to international friction. The areas of friction would themselves be greatly reduced by the preliminary achievement of largely self-contained national organisations. "What a strange economic process!' "our objector may retort. "In fact, your method of settling international trade is largely to eliminate it."

Once again we must tell him that he is still gripped by the school of poverty economics; that today the problem is not how to eke out the exiguous resources of mankind by a free flow of the thin trickle of international trade; rather the problem of today is to release within each nation the vast resources of modern industrial production. Thereby we shall approach as near as possible in organisation to the self-contained, and will withdraw in large degree from the mad scramble to dump surplus production on the markets of the world, which will then find an outlet in the home market.

If our objectors must persist in their poverty economics of the last century, let them in practice continue for the next ten years, as they have in the last, constant and humble attendants at international conferences, begging an impoverished world to throw a few pennyworth of concessions into the outstretched palm of a down-and-out Britain.

For our own part, we prefer the effort of self-help and of national reorganisation, which at a later date will lead to Britain's reappearance in the conclaves of the nations, not as a supplicant, but as a world leader.

Chapter 9 - Fascism and its Neighbours

FOREIGN POLICY

Our foreign policy should also be the subject of a book in itself, but the main principles may here be stated very briefly.

The measures of national reconstruction already described involve automatically a change in our foreign policy. We should be less prone to anxious interference in everybody else's affairs, and more concentrated on the resources of our own country and Empire. Wherever opportunity arose for furthering the interests of British trade, we should seize that chance, and to that end would reorganise the Diplomatic and Consular Service. Henceforth their activities would be more directed to practical commercial questions, and less to the tangled skein of European politics and animosities. The mere fact of our international concentration would tend to relieve us from some of our anxiety over, and participation in, the troubles and turmoil of the Continent.

This does not by any means imply that we would withdraw from the world scene and not exert ourselves in the cause of World Peace. We would certainly use all existing machinery to that end, including the machinery of the League of Nations. We do not believe that this machinery, as at present constituted, is effective. But the Fascist method is not to destroy, but to use and transform existing machinery for different ends.

It must never be forgotten that the League of Nations is a piece of machinery, and not a human entity. Like other machines, it is subject to the will of those who operate it. Hitherto the drivers of that machine have driven it in a direction, and worked it in a way, which we consider to be usually futile and often dangerous; but, as realists, we are not prepared on that account to seek the destruction of the machine. Rather we seek, by different methods and direction, to use it for different purposes. Above all, in the deliberations of that body and in other international affairs, we should call a halt to the flabby surrender of every British interest which has characterised the past decade, and has reduced this nation to the position of a meddlesome old-lady holding the baby for the world. We should seek peace and conciliation with every nation, but we do not believe that every bad debt of mankind should be liquidated with a cheque signed by Britain.

The future of European peace must depend on the co-operation of the Great Powers. To this end it is of importance that the Great Powers should be of like mind. The existence of Fascist Governments in all great countries is the surest guarantee of European Peace. In the first place, they will be composed of men who know what war means from experience of the last war and are, consequently, determined to prevent a recurrence of that catastrophe. In the second place, they will be indissolubly united by their determination to prevent a catastrophe which can only lead to the triumph of their common enemy, Communism. A quarrel between Fascist Governments would be a betrayal of our cause to the enemy and any Fascist contemplating war is a traitor to Fascism as well as to humanity. Fascist Governments united in the great Brotherhood of Fascism could and should build the enduring peace of Europe on a stable basis.

It is necessary to reconstruct the League of Nations in accord with the requirements of reality, which predicate the effective Leadership of the Great Powers. To deny that Leadership is to deny both the spiritual and material realities of modern Europe. Yet it has been denied in the present procedure of the League where a host of small Powers and interests in the final frenzy of democratic ideology have been permitted to paralyse effective action. The effective Leadership of the Great Powers must be established within a reconstituted League of Nations in which the small Powers will have effective representation, but will not be able to obstruct the necessary measures of European reconstruction.

It will be the task of Fascist Europe to eliminate the risk of war by removing the causes of war. The economic causes of war, which are by far the most powerful factors in that disaster, will be reduced to the vanishing point by the policy already described in the previous chapter. It will be necessary further to revise at least economic boundaries which have constituted uneconomic units in Europe with a constant tendency to disturb the peace. All nations also must be granted adequate supplies of raw materials and a full opportunity to build an economic life of their own. This will not be difficult in a world which is producing a super-abundance of raw materials and is vainly seeking a market for them. In this respect, as in many others, the problems of plenty are easier of solution than the problems of poverty once the will and the power is present to grapple with them. That will and power can only come from a Fascist Europe united by the Brotherhood of Fascism and the common determination to preserve and to elevate European culture in a higher and greater world morality.

ARMAMENTS.

Disarmament has so far proved impracticable owing to the sense of universal insecurity which a Fascist Europe alone can overcome. Nations have been divided by different psychologies and methods, and still more by commercial rivalries and memories of that "triumph "of Democratic statesmanship, the Peace of 1918. Under Fascism the outlook of the new European generation will be expressed in a closer synthesis of nations, commercial rivalries will be diminished and controlled and legacies of the unhappy past will be buried in a united effort of new European culture to build a new civilisation. The sense of insecurity will be removed with the reasons for insecurity and Disarmament will become for the first time a practical proposition. Disarmament which is universal and proportionate leaves the relative strength of nations the same and increases their real security.

It is true that nations can still fight whether armed or unarmed and that in the event of Disarmament the best equipped nations have the advantage if war should occur. But this consideration should not unduly disturb a nation with leading chemical industries, the largest merchant fleet in the world and a pre-eminent aptitude for the Air which, under Fascism, would be developed into a leading place. Disarmament itself is no guarantee of peace. For that we must rely on an entirely new psychology and we may well ask where Europe can discover that new psychology except in Fascism. But Disarmament, if universal, is a definite step towards Peace and we should strenuously strive to secure it both as a contribution to Peace and as a relief from a heavy and unproductive burden. We should, therefore, be prepared to take the lead in Disarmament proposals, provided they were universal, and not confined to this country. But we would not consent to a unilateral reduction which would render Britain helpless in the menacing dangers of the present world; a crime of which all the Old Parties have been guilty.

On the other hand, with the best possible expert advice we would radically overhaul our present system of defence. It is a strange mind which meticulously contends for exact parity in every naval category with a friendly power like America, which is more than three thousand miles away, but is willing to accept a two-and-a-half to one inferiority in the Air from another friendly power which is only twenty miles away. We would submit to the analysis of scientific examination, rather than to sentiment, the whole question of Imperial defence, which we believe today to be guided by vested interest and tradition as much as by the ascertained requirements of defence in modern conditions.

The arrival of the Air factor has altered fundamentally the position of these Islands, and the consequences of that factor have never yet been realised by the older generation of politicians. We will immediately raise the air strength of Britain to the level of the strongest power in Europe. Successive governments have criminally weakened our air force and exposed this country to the gravest danger. I have never ceased to attack this mad policy since the war and under Fascism it will immediately be revised. While the armaments of other powers persist, we must be able to defend ourselves both in the air and on the sea. There is no greater danger to the nation than defences strong enough to invite attack, but too weak to resist it. Socialists have advocated complete unilateral disarmament which would leave us at the mercy of an armed world. Conservatives have pursued the, if possible, more dangerous policy of pretending to maintain armaments which, in fact, were ill-equipped or inadequate. The country has been lulled into a false sense of security to tolerate a policy which it would never have accepted if it had been appraised of the facts. We will certainly seek peace and Disarmament and we will secure these great blessings for mankind in the Fascist Europe of the future. Meanwhile, we must save Britain from the ignoble and defenceless position to which the treachery of the Old Parties has reduced her.

In such a study as this, covering much ground that is entirely novel and demanding space for that purpose, it is impossible to deal with world policy in terms other than the general.

In general, we would seek peace and conciliation, and are prepared to take the lead in these subjects. Too long has Britain, even in this sphere, been a hesitant attendant on other nations.

Our main policy quite frankly is a policy of "Britain First", but our very preoccupation with internal reconstruction is some guarantee that at least we shall never pursue the folly of an aggressive Imperialism. It will never be necessary to stimulate the steady temper of Britain in the task of rebuilding our own country by appeals to flamboyant national sentiment in foreign affairs. We shall mind our own business, but we will help in the organisation of world peace, as part of that business.

Chapter 10 - Finance, Industry and Science

THE disastrous effects of a financial system unrelated to national policy, and indifferent to a national economic plan, were examined at the conclusion of our economic analysis. The problem of our financial system remains one of the most difficult and delicate with which the nation is faced. On the one hand, that financial system, in the services which it supplies to the world, is a source of wealth and of revenue to the nation. A traditional and almost hereditary skill has been acquired over generations in the City of London, which enables it to carry on a highly complicated business which no other country has mastered. Only a fool would be anxious to rush in from outside with rough-and-ready measures of interference with a machinery so delicate. On the other hand, it must be recognised that, in recent years, many activities of the City of London have been disastrous to the interests of the nation.

In particular, they have shaken to the foundations the great producers' interests on which the strength and stability of the nation must ultimately rest, and the depression of which today is involving even the City in the national loss. In every struggle between producer and financial interest in recent years, the latter power has been triumphant to the detriment of the national interest. In fact, we have within the nation a power, largely controlled by alien elements, which arrogates to itself a power above the State, and has used that influence to drive flaccid governments of all political parties along the high road to national disaster. No State can tolerate within its body the irresponsible superiority of such a power, nor the policy inimical to every productive interest which it has pursued.

Not only has this been the case, but it must also be admitted that financial leadership in the City is markedly at a discount. Our Banking system is based on mammoth money-lending concerns, in which the aspiring employee's biggest responsibility lies in permitting or refusing minor overdrafts. From positions as Branch Managers, with no conception beyond that of detail and no vision beyond the cash-counter, men are promoted to responsible head-office appointments in which they handle wide aspects of the nation's financial policy. A man may be excellently equipped to decide whether Jones, Brown & Company shall be allowed an extended sanction for a further three months; but this very capacity suggests that he is unfitted for dealing with major issues.

Superimposed upon the head-office staff, which is the nearest thing to a responsible banking organ, each of the joint stock banks supports a board of directors elected almost entirely for their ornamental qualities.

Unfortunately, such a system contributes little to the building up of a constructive financial organism. The publication of the Macmillan Report disclosed the fact that our banks had advanced to the money and stock markets a volume of credit as great as the whole amount advanced to the cotton, wool, silk, linen, jute, iron, steel, shipbuilding and engineering trades. They were supporting speculation, and short-term lending abroad, rather than assisting in the constructive work for which the financial system is primarily intended.

Their policy, if policy it can be called, severely damaged the country's great producing interests. Yet it is upon production that, in the last analysis, our stability must rest. Even now, when bankers can borrow at a half of 1 per cent., and money is freely said to be "unusable", "abundant", "plentiful", "a drug on the market", industrialists must still pay 5 per cent, for their overdrafts. Even now the necessity for financial support of industry is not realised.

Finance chose the path of least resistance and of easiest reward by lending at high interest to Central Europe. Such a course promised large profits at an early date, and the City could not see the effects of the neglect of British industry. The bankers did not realise that they were setting industry in competition with almost insolvent foreign borrowers, who would promise uneconomic interest rather than go without support.

It is probable that the bankers would now recognise the fundamental error of their late proceedings. They acted inimically towards productive industry, and they were themselves involved in the cataclysm. Their interests, they now have every reason to realise, are identical - if properly considered – with those of the State.

It is different when we consider the Bank of England, and the power of the private banking houses. Here we are dealing with a great tradition of public activity, founded on a policy eminently suited to the nineteenth-century economics, of poverty. During that period foreign lending assumed an enormous importance, through the necessity for consolidating our position and assuring our supplies of materials. Now all raw materials are superabundant; the necessity is no longer so vital. But the power of the great private bankers continues undiminished.

Through these houses was conducted the bulk of our foreign lending in the past. One need only instance the South American flotation's of the house of Rothschild to realise how enormous was their scope. For this purpose a huge connection must be built up, internationally as well as at home, and the organisation soon became very efficient, but also very costly. It was desirable, in the interests of these financial houses, to keep the machine at work, to feed the financial connections with fresh supplies of foreign lending.

All international banking is founded on the maintenance of stable currencies. Already, soon after the War, the supremacy of London was threatened by the rise of New York as a monetary centre. The United States were on the Gold Standard, and they had acquired during the War an enormous potential surplus of payments. The work of American bankers in Europe was astonishingly able and constructive - a fine example was Dillon Read's participation in reorganising the steel industry of Germany. At that time it was not recognised that, in all international banking, connections count for more than mere capacity. To the London houses it appeared that our currency, being unstable, obstructed the recovery of our financial prestige. It is human nature to believe that your own interests are those of the nations at large. The banking houses concerned arc represented in great force among the Directors of the Bank of England. It is obvious from whence the pressure came for our disastrous return to gold in 1925. Before and since that time, in the sacred interests of a supposedly impregnable currency, industry has been sacrificed and the fixed-income owner enriched.

Beyond all these forces stand the great interests of the money market, the Acceptance and Discount houses whose interests are wholly and frankly monetary. In Lombard Street money is bought and sold like a commodity; there is no consideration of whither and whence. Except under pressure, as in the early days of War Loan conversion, the money market can take no heed of other than monetary considerations. It has no ear for the voice of industry, nor yet for any form of national interest. Its power is almost wholly international, and it is wielded by hands few of which are British. It must be a fundamental axiom of Fascism that high finance, like every other interest within the State, must be subordinated to the policy of the State, and must serve the welfare of the nation as a whole.

In adopting this position, for the first time in British politics, after the weak surrender of all parties to the power of finance, the British Government would have the overwhelming support of the mass of the people, both worker and employer, whose productive efforts have been frustrated by the policy of high finance. The attitude of the City itself will determine the need, or otherwise, for intervention. Indeed, within the City itself considerable support could be found for this position from genuine British and patriotic elements, who are not enmeshed in the trammels of foreign finance. Let us hope that it may prove possible, by cooperation with such elements in the City, to secure the co-operation of British finance in a planned economy of national reconstruction. Otherwise, the Gordian Knot must be cut.

INDUSTRY

Many of our recent troubles have arisen from the fact that our financial system has grown up in a tradition of international rather than British finance. The business of the great finance houses has been largely foreign business rather than the supply of finance to British industry. This tradition has a natural origin in the fact that British industry originally itself financed new developments chiefly from its own resources and reserves, and without much recourse to the City.

However, that epoch has long passed away, and urgent measures of big-scale rationalisation seek financial aid only to find the whole practice, tradition and interest of the City engaged in international finance. The big banks have developed also a tradition of rigorously refraining from industrial enterprise, and content themselves with advances upon collateral security, irrespective of the purpose to which the borrower will devote the credit. These practices are, of course, in strong contradistinction to the practice of foreign banks, notably the German, who have long been partners in German industrial enterprise. With traditional aptitude for such business, acquired from long experience, they can appoint skilled directors to the boards of new enterprises, and are partners and participants in all the varying experiences of German industry.

Such practice, of course, has its dangers. In the period of industrial depression superimposed, as far as they were concerned, upon the problems of reparation, many German banks have found themselves in difficulties. This is no argument against the system; it proves, rather, the need for the safeguards of Corporate structure in the interests of bankers as well as industrial producers.

While it may not be possible or desirable to translate the British banking system into an industrial banking system, it is vitally necessary to provide a banking machinery for the re-equipment of British industry. Hitherto, Government has washed its hands of one of the major problems of the age, and has abdicated in favour of the Bank of England, which in equipment, training and tradition was manifestly unsuited to the task, while on general grounds of administrative principle the Central Bank does not seem to be the appropriate instrument for the details of industrial reconstruction.

The result, after three years' experience, has so far produced no noticeable improvement in the conditions of British industry. Hitherto the power of finance in industry has been used, not so much to produce efficiency and to promote new enterprises, as to maintain concerns which were demonstrably rotten, long after their economic basis had gone, in the hope of ultimately liquidating ill judged credits which were frozen.

A further necessity of our system, hitherto quite neglected, is that for intermediate credit. This was emphasised by the Macmillan Committee, and was intended to cover instalment selling and the purchase of larger units, such as ships, against deferred payment. In addition, it would cover large contracts, such as the construction of railways, docks, harbours, etc., for which capital is not productive soon enough to be used as an ordinary investment. A system, covering this field could also be extended to cover small companies, the finance of which is not large enough to justify the cost of a public issue.

This aspect of finance is neglected by our present system; in this respect, as in others, the older method has failed. Against it we set the systematic plan of Corporate organisation. For the re-equipment of industry we propose a National Investment Board on which the constructive minds of British banking and finance would be invited to serve. This Board would also control and co-ordinate for productive purposes all investments which arc at present made by Government and local authorities, such as the work of the Public Loans Board, the investments of the Post Office Savings Bank, and other bodies.

It would be charged with the development of public works of national importance on an economic basis in times of depression and unemployment. Such works have been the mark of efficient and virile government in every period of history. They have been continually blocked in England in recent years by the school of thought which is willing to raise loans of millions for the development of foreign countries, but sees financial catastrophe in any effort to divert such loans to the reconstruction of Britain and to the employment of our own people.

Nothing is more humiliating than to watch the successful efforts of a relatively poor country like Italy to provide useful work in place of unemployment benefit, while the Government of powerful Britain stands impotent before the problem, and continues to pay out something for nothing. The details of such works will not be repeated, as I have so often covered this ground, notably at the time of my resignation from the Labour Government. Our policy would always be to give useful work to the unemployed, rather than pay out benefit pending their re-absorption in reconstructed industry. Foremost among such works must come the re-housing of our slum population, whose condition today is a disgrace to our civilisation, at a time when thousands in the building trade are unemployed.

The National Investment Board working in conjunction with the National Corporation of Industry, would at last succeed in relating the activities of British finance to the needs of British industry. It would be faced with an immense task, ranging from the reconstruction of services such as transport, coal, electricity, power in all forms, to the re-equipment of competitive industry on modern lines. Also, in co-operation with the Corporative system, which would seek to raise wages and the standard of life, it would be charged with holding a proper balance between consumption and saving, which is one of the more important questions of national policy. At present these things are left to chance; no system of regulation exists in this important sphere, with very bad results. It is idle, by saving, to create fresh capital to provide plant and factories to produce for a market which is already oversupplied; on the other hand, it is dangerous and uneconomic to raise consuming power at the expense of saving to a point where capital for industrial re-equipment cannot be found.

The solution of this problem is a matter of continual adjustment of the balance between spending and saving, which can only be done by co-operation between the Corporative system, which seeks, inter alia, to increase purchasing power, and the financial system, which is charged with the task of finding fresh capital for industry from national savings. Any such scheme for industrial and financial co-operation in national reconstruction would probably be opposed to the utmost by some interests in the City, whose foreign commitments conflict with British interests. If their opposition were carried to effective lengths, the active intervention of Government for their suppression would be necessary. We do not seek intervention for intervention's sake, in the manner of the meddlesome Socialist. But Fascism will not hesitate to act when the State interests are threatened, and the action of such a power will be decisive.

In this sphere, as in others, the decisive factor will be the existence of a modern movement permeating and gripping all elements of national life, irrespective of class or interest, and uniting them in the Corporate conception. There will be no room in Britain for those who do not accept the principle "All for the State and the State for all."

SCIENCE, INVENTION AND RESEARCH

Allied to our financial and industrial institutions will be a greatly extended system of scientific and industrial research. The development of new industries must rest upon science and invention; their development is essential if we are easily to effect the great transition, rendered needful by our declining exports, from production for export to production for the domestic market.

A Department of Scientific Research already exists, but its scope is limited and its funds are exiguous. Like medical research, which might at any moment, if properly supported, rid mankind of many scourges, so scientific research, if properly supported, might revive great industries such as the mines of this country by the development of such processes as the derivation of oil fuel from coal.

The great possibilities of science are not deemed worthy of proper support in this curious muddle of Old Gang politics. Not only is scientific research inadequately supported in this country; the individual inventor is often driven abroad by the total absence of financial support to carry a proved invention through from the proved experiment to the open market stage.

No country produces a greater wealth of inventive talent, and no country more recklessly squanders that talent; yet no country is so peculiarly dependent in our present position upon the development of such aptitude for the advance of new industries.

Therefore, far more powerful machinery of government must be created, not only for the purpose of scientific research and the fostering of invention, but also for the carrying through of new inventions from the proved experiment to the point where public support may be sought. Millions of public money have been wasted in recent years through dubious companies floating doubtful inventions on the Stock Exchange and fleecing an ignorant public unprotected by the examination and safeguards of Government. The public must be protected, and the resources thus wasted must be mobilised for the genuine work of industrial reconstruction.

We propose, therefore, that the machinery of the National Investment Board should be linked to that of scientific research. Thus, for the first time, science would be properly supported, not only by official discrimination between the genuine and the bogus, but also by financial machinery designed to support the genuine discovery, and to translate it into industrial achievement. We must call in the new world of science to redress the balance of the old world of industry. We must found a Corporate State on the wealth of scientific and technical skill which no other nation possesses in equal measure. By such machinery we would link the National Corporation, which is not only a synthesis of all industrial experience, but also a Council planning under Government the general economic development of the nation, with machinery which mobilised our scientific resources and supported them by measures of practical financial assistance.

Chapter 11 - The Nation's Finance

THE question of currency policy has already been considerably discussed. That question now engages the attention of statesmen who have for long neglected it. We believe that only a stable price-level can predicate the conditions in which industrial reconstruction can be carried through; and that stable price-level, in its turn, can only be secured by a rational monetary system.

On the other hand, we believe that monetary stability is the beginning, and by no means the end, of the problem; and that there is no small danger in the universal rush towards credit quackery on the part of senior politicians, who, a few years ago, refused to admit the existence of a credit problem. Currency questions should be seen in proper perspective to the whole. Money is as essential to industrial life as the carburettor to a motor engine, but it is not the whole machine. The adjustment of the carburettor will not solve our problems if the cylinders are still cracked.

MONETARY POLICY

Our monetary policy can be defined very briefly. So long as the deflationary tendency continues in the Gold Standard countries, we believe in a managed currency for this country. If we have to choose, we prefer a fluctuating exchange to a fluctuating internal price-level. We should consequently aim, in present conditions, at a stable price level; but seek, so far as possible, to extend the existing area of nations who have attached their currency to sterling. We should under no consideration return to the old Gold Standard nor consider the fixing of our Exchange at the previous parity. The rationalisation of gold supplies throughout the world may secure in effect a managed currency which may be related to gold but aims at a stable level of commodity prices. Such an arrangement would suit our requirements but any return to the old automatic Gold Standard would be fatal to reconstruction. We must devise a managed currency which is designed to serve the interests of the British Producer and to provide without any measure of inflation the credit necessary to a high production system. Through the Corporate State new credit would be directed to productive purposes alone and would be balanced by a greater production which would prevent any tendency towards an inflation of prices.

It should not be forgotten that we have means to enforce our ends in monetary policy not only within the confines of our own Nation. Some 70 per cent, of the annual new gold supply of the world is produced within the British Empire, and if the gold reserves of the Empire countries were pooled, they would amount to some £230 millions.

If Empire countries were willing to pool their gold reserves and to establish a statutory monopoly in a central bank to acquire our annual gold production, we should dominate the gold position of the world. The power would rest with us, either to enforce the rationalisation of the gold system, or ultimately to drive every country off the Gold Standard.

It is time that the latent power of our great strength was used to overcome some of the follies which are now wrecking the industrial and financial system of the world.

TAXATION AND ECONOMY

In general we believe, as already intimated, that the balance of trade is far more important than the temporary balancing of a Budget. Nothing is more futile than to balance the Budget by means of taxation and economy, without corresponding measures to balance trade. It is trite to say that revenue depends on industry, and that the decline of industry means a decline of revenue; but that fact has been consistently ignored. Nothing is more foolish than to pile up the burden of taxation, and by small economy to harass and to bully the unemployed while allowing the industrial situation, which is responsible for the financial difficulty, to drift towards a still more complete collapse. For this reason we have always opposed the policy of "cuts." Incompetent politicians of all parties have tried, by such measures, to make the poor pay for the failure of Governments to produce a constructive policy. It is the duty of Parliament to make them think again - and think harder.

INDUSTRIAL RECONSTRUCTION

The prime necessity of the present is a policy of industrial reconstruction, which will increase revenue returns through the medium of trade revival, and will thus make possible both a reduction of taxation and an improvement in working class standards.

Lord Rothermere states the cold truth in face of the failure of all Governments to produce a policy of industrial reconstruction when he says that "this country cannot support a burden of taxation – local or national - of more than 50 per cent, of what it is at present called upon to bear ".

A nation in the grip of our present trade depression cannot support indefinitely the present burden of taxation without some operation of the law of diminishing returns, which will lead in the end to financial collapse. In fact, we have to choose between the effort of industrial reconstruction and the passive acceptance of a vast reduction of standards of living.

We believe that the industrial measures outlined already would relatively soon lead to increasing revenue returns, and the end of financial difficulties. If, prior to the effects of reconstruction being felt in greater revenue returns, it was necessary to meet the situation by measures of economy and taxation, we would lay down certain clear-cut principles to that end. When fresh taxation was required, we should turn first to those who have benefited most from recent policy, namely, the great rentier class, the owners of fixed-interest bearing securities whose purchasing power has been doubled in the past decade. It is not beyond administrative possibility to devise special taxation for those who enjoy unearned income from fixed interest bearing security; on the ground of equity it is desirable that they should bear any additional burden which has to be borne.

We should also turn to hereditary wealth for such purposes. While we regard as part of the legitimate urge to private enterprise the desire of a man to hand on to his children the wealth which he himself has created, we do not regard it as desirable that such wealth should be handed on from generation to generation by people who have contributed nothing to its creation. Such a system is not a stimulus, but a burden, to private enterprise. It actually encourages idleness and the development of a parasitic class.

We are definitely against such transmission of hereditary wealth from generation to generation as piles up a dead weight of interest on industry and the nation in order to maintain a relatively small class in idleness. It will be necessary to discriminate between different categories of hereditary wealth ; for instance, it is highly undesirable that hereditary farming should be broken up by imposts which prevent a son, on the death of his Father, from working the land on which he was brought up. But the general principle of Fascism will be that accumulated wealth may be justified only from one generation to another. A man should be allowed to work not only for himself but for his children. He should be permitted, as at present, to leave a proportion of the money he makes to his family. But it is for the State to decide whether transmission to a further generation is justified by service. If, therefore, a family fortune is to be preserved, each succeeding generation must contribute by national service (not necessarily commercial) to its maintenance. By this principle Fascism will retain the incentive of a man to work not only for himself but for his children, but will rid the nation of the dead weight of usury which distorts the productive processes of the country and cripples industrial development.

Our aim throughout is to rid productive industry of its

financial burden. Successive governments have paid lip service to this principle and in the De-Rating Act the first pathetic advance was made towards its translation into practical politics. But, if the principle is clearly recognised, the effects are far more profound. Hitherto the holder of ordinary shares, who is the true risk bearer in industrial enterprise, has been treated as the holder of an "unearned income" and taxed on the same basis as the investor in debentures, bonds and other forms of money lending. Private industrialists, too, have been in the same position; though they carried the risk, they have been penalised if their incomes increased; there has been nothing to encourage the salaried man to take the risk of enterprise on his own account. The whole procedure is illogical, and calculated to discourage the enterprise upon which our industrial future depends. We must distinguish, in taxing earned incomes, between the enterprising and the cautious; in taxing unearned incomes, between the producer and the usurer.

The only means of enforcing economy is the constitution of strong government. Real economy means efficiency. The so-called economies of today are usually the fruits of inefficiency. The power ruthlessly to cut down the redundant, and to resist the consequent clamour of vested interests, can only rest with a government stronger in its whole constitution than the so-called democratic governments of today. In the actual administration problem in which economy resides, only such forces of government as we have described can function with success.

INCREASE OF REVENUE

We indicate the general principles by which we believe that economy can be secured and taxation should be raised when such measures are necessary: but the fact cannot be over-stressed that we are not a movement of taxation but of reconstruction. We come to these conclusions, not because we are demagogues, for we advocate many things which are novel, and therefore unpopular; but our whole economic analysis leads us to the belief that the real solution is to reconstruct industry, and not to diminish purchasing power by taxation. We believe that an increasing revenue derived from reviving industry is the real way out. We shall not win through by putting the patient to bed on a starvation diet, but by taking him out into the fields of effort for exertion and for the rebuilding of muscle and constitution. The former is the remedy of the eternal old woman in government; the latter is the remedy of manhood.

Chapter 12 - Conclusion

THE case advanced in these pages covers, not only a new political policy, but also a new conception of life. In our view, these purposes can only be achieved by the creation of a modern movement invading every sphere of national life. To succeed, such a movement must represent the organised revolt of the young manhood of Britain against things as they are. The enemy is the "Old Gang " of our present political system. No matter what their Party label, the old parliamentarians have proved themselves to be all the same; no matter what policy they are elected to carry out, their policy when elected is invariably the same. That policy is a policy of subservience to sectional interests and of national lethargy.

At the end of the War, they found Britain raised by the efforts of the young generation to a pinnacle or power and of greatness. Their rule of fourteen years has surrendered that position, and has reduced this country, at home and abroad, to a low and dangerous condition. Again we raise the standard of youth and challenge that betrayal. The first attempt was the formation of the New Party in 1931, which attracted a powerful body of adherents throughout the country. From the outset, the New Party met with a concentrated attack of organised misrepresentation and ridicule from the old Parliamentarians and the Press of the great vested interests by which they are served. As a result, its policy and aims were never known or discussed by the public.

It was temporarily overwhelmed in the General Election of October, 1931, by the last great bluff of the Old Gangs in the formation of a National Government. A blank cheque was given by the electorate to a government of "united muttons", which openly combined, for the first time, every failure of post-war politics. Every Old Gang politician deserted his particular variety of sinking ship, and scrambled aboard the new lifeboat. Only the rump of Labour leadership was left behind - a collection of men whose intellectual calibre was deemed by their late colleagues unworthy of inclusion in the new combination.

THE FAILURE OF NATIONAL GOVERNMENT

The National Government had no programme when they started, and they have no programme today. Their leaders had not foreseen the crisis of 1931 until it overwhelmed them, and indeed derided its possibility; but the public was assured that our troubles would automatically be overcome by the mere fact of the new combination of the old forces. The crisis, as well as the heart of the electorate, was to melt before the sudden embraces of a few old gentlemen who had spent the previous half-century in abusing each other.

Unfortunately, facts are sterner than the emotions of democracy. They have soon proved that some further action was required than has emerged as yet from the Old Gang honeymoon. In such an atmosphere, every appeal to thought, to reason, to effort and to action was naturally defeated. Our constructive programme was derided and dismissed, only later to be adopted in part by the National Government - but in so small a degree, so tardily and in such muddled fashion, as to render it entirely ineffective.

For all this we make no complaint whatsoever; such experience is merely the classic first phase of a Modern movement. Actually we fared far better at our first attempt than any of the modern movements which have been founded and which have come to power in other countries since the War. The Italian Fascists were more utterly defeated in the election of 1919, about three years before they came into power. Their leader polled only 5,000 votes against the 100,000 of his Old Gang opponent - a result only some 20 per cent, as good as that which I was afforded by the people of Stoke-on-Trent in the election of 1931.

If we turn to the case of the German Nazis, we find that they were routed again and again by national combinations of their Old Gang before they approached power. It is only natural that nations in crisis should seek the easy and the normal way of escape. It is only natural that they should trust the well-known and venerable figures in politics until these are found unworthy of trust and unsuitable to a dynamic age. Only then, with the new determination born of despair, great nations turn to new forces and to new men.

The first result of crisis in every nation has always been a national combination of "the united muttons." Only after their failure, the modern movement begins its inevitable advance. The aim of such a movement must be revolutionary in the fundamental changes which it seeks to secure. But all these changes can be achieved by legal and by peaceful means, and it is our ardent desire so to secure them. Whether they will be thus achieved depends, chiefly, upon the rapidity with which new ideas are accepted in this country.

To drift much longer, to muddle through much further, is to run the risk of collapse. In such a situation, new ideas will not come peacefully; they will come violently, as they have come elsewhere. In the final economic crisis to which neglect may lead, argument, reason, persuasion, vanish and organised force alone prevails. In such a situation, the eternal protagonists in the history of all modern crises must struggle for the mastery of the State. Either Fascism or Communism emerges victorious; if it be the latter, the story of Britain is told.

Anyone who argues that in such a situation the normal instruments of government, such as police and army, can be used effectively, has studied neither the European history of his own time nor the realities of the present situation. In the highly technical struggle for the modern State in crisis, only the technical organisations of Fascism and of Communism have ever prevailed, or, in the nature of the case, can prevail. Governments and Parties which have relied on the normal instruments of government (which are not constituted for such purposes) have fallen easy and ignoble victims to the forces of anarchy. If, therefore, such a situation arises in Britain, we shall prepare to meet the anarchy of Communism with the organised force of Fascism; but we do not seek that struggle, and for the sake of the nation we desire to avert it. Only when we see the feeble surrender to menacing problems, the fatuous optimism which again and again has been disproved, the spineless drift towards disaster, do we feel it necessary to organise for such a contingency.

Action, even now, might avert it; but can anyone, after an experience of post-war politics, hope for such action from existing political parties, from the men who lead them, or, indeed, from the existing political system. The whole constitution, composition, tradition, psychology and outlook of the older political parties inhibit them from facing the problems of the modern age. Nothing has yet overcome the modern problem in other countries, or in our view can overcome it in this country, except that phenomenon of the modern period, which is the modern movement of organised Fascism.

It was often urged strongly upon me that I could find acceptance for many of the ideas set out in this book within one of the existing parties, and that it is folly to attempt the great labour of creating new machinery for purposes which could be achieved by existing machinery.

Such an argument betrays a complete misunderstanding of the problem and the history of this period. It would have been equally futile to tell an Italian Fascist that he could achieve the renaissance of Italy through the Parliament of Giolitti, or a German Nazi that he should cease his struggle and should seek to persuade the opponents whose failure created the necessity for his organisation. New ideas have never come, in the modern world, except from the new and organised reality.

In Great Britain, salvation has not come, in fourteen years, from the old parties, and it will not come. They are not alive to crisis; they are not organised to meet it; and their mind and psychology are unsuited to it. We cannot compromise with them, for "their ways are not our ways and their gods are not our gods."

It is true that within the old parties and even within the old Parliament are many young men whose real place is with us, and who sympathise with our ideas. The real political division of the past decade has not been a division of parties, but a division of generations. At any time in the past few years it would have been possible to form a government of broadly homogeneous ideas from the men over fifty years of age, and a corresponding government from the men under fifty years of age. It was left to the older generation to demonstrate the truth of this view in the formation of a National Government.

In the case of the younger generation, the machinery of Party Government, which is controlled by the old, has made any such development impossible. The power of that party machine has crushed all attempts to secure a natural alignment in British politics. Nevertheless, within all political parties potential Fascists are to be found among young men who are well known in party politics, and still more among the rank and file.

Before we can draw such support, which would mean the collapse of the old political system and the achievement of a new national unity, we have to advance much further on the road to victory. We have to discover, as we have already discovered, new men, and we have to create a new force from nothing except the will of the mass of people to victory.

It is thus that every Fascist movement has arrived at power - not by combinations of men drawn from the old political system, but by the discovery of new men who come from nowhere, and by the creation of a new force which is free from the trammels of the past. Except for a few leading figures who broke from the old political system and staked all on the creation of the new, the makers of Fascism in all countries had never been heard of before the arrival of that movement.

For our purposes, therefore, we cannot rely on well-known names and figures. Few of them will take the risks of so great an adventure as the creation of a modern movement, and we cannot expect them to take those risks. If we are to be true to our faith, we must ourselves take risks which most men will not take, and must stake our all on a mission which in its early stages must be lonely.

THE COMING STRUGGLE

In the coming struggle, we shall have the imposing things of the world against us, and much of its material strength. The great names of politics, the power of party machinery and Press, will oppose us with a concentrated barrage of misrepresentation, or with a well-organised boycott, as they have opposed us in the past and as they opposed all such movements as this in every country. But we have on our side forces which have carried such movements to victory throughout the world. We have in unison in our cause the economic facts and the spiritual tendencies of our age. These are the forces which in so many countries in recent history have smashed all the pomp and panoply of the old political systems and have enthroned new creeds in power.

Britain is different, we are told (and certainly we invite Britain to do things in a different way). Germany was different from Italy, they said a short time ago, and they were right in that the gulf between the Latin and the Teuton is greater than the gulf which separates either of them from the Englishman. But in the hour of crisis that phenomenon of the modern age, which is an organised, Fascist movement, leapt the gulf between Latin and Teuton and reappeared in an almost identical form.

Fascism today has become a world-wide movement, invading every country in the hour of crisis as the only alternative to a destructive Communism. We must remember that, in the long course of history, all great movements which swept the Continent have come in the end to these shores. They have come, but in very different form and character. We, too, seek to create the Modern movement in Britain in a form very different from Continental forms, with characteristics which are peculiarly British and in a manner which will strive to avoid the excesses and the horrors of Continental struggle.

Whether these aims can be realised depends upon whether Britain will wake soon or late. Can we again show the political genius which translated the great movement that ravaged the Continent at the end of the eighteenth century into the sanity and the balance of the forces which later carried the great Reform Bill in Britain, and which no other country could have conceived or have produced? The new order, which was born on the Continent amid a welter of blood, was then brought to birth in Britain by a method and by a policy which were characteristic of our ordered greatness. Why then, we ask, should the arrival - and the inevitable arrival - of the great forces of the new age in Britain be heralded by violence? Has Britain still the political wisdom and the national determination to avert it? Is the appeal to reason to be all in vain? Must we drift helplessly to the arbitrament of force?

For our part, we appeal to our countrymen to take action while there is time, and to carry the changes which are necessary by the legal and constitutional methods which are available. If, on the other hand, every appeal to reason is futile in the future, as it has been in the immediate past, and this Empire is allowed to drift until collapse and anarchy supervene, we shall not shrink from that final conclusion, and will organise to stand between the State and ruin.

We are accused of organising to promote violence. That accusation is untrue. It is true that we are organised to protect our meetings as far as possible from violence;. and very necessary that organisation has proved in practice. Already in this country we have a condition in which free speech is a thing of the past.

The leaders of the old political parties creep in by back doors, under police protection, to well picketed meetings which would otherwise be broken up by the organised violence of Socialist and Communist extremists. We have thrown open our meetings to the public, and after the meetings we have exercised the Englishman's right to walk through the streets of our great cities. When we have been attacked, we have hit back, and as a result I have been subject to the farce of being summoned to a police court for assault by Reds who came to break up our meetings by force; and who ran howling, when counter force was employed, for the protection of the police and the law which they had previously derided.

The great majority of our meetings, even in the early days, were peaceful. In fact, although little else appeared in the Press, only two out of some hundred meetings which I addressed at the Election ended in a fight; and the return visit, even to Glasgow, was strangely peaceful. Nevertheless, when we are confronted by red terror, we are certainly organised to meet force by force, and will always do our utmost to smash it. The bully of the streets has gone too long unchallenged. We shall continue to exercise the right of free speech, and will do our utmost to defend it.

Emphatically, this does not mean that we seek violence. On the contrary, we seek our aims by methods which are both legal and constitutional, and we appeal to our country, by taking action in time, to avert the possibility of violence. If the situation of violence is to be averted, the Old Gang Government must be overthrown and effective measures must be adopted before the situation has gone too far. The enemy today is the Old Gang of present parliamentarianism. The enemy of tomorrow, if their rule persists much longer, will be the Communist Party. The Old Gangs are the Architects of disaster, the Communists only its executors. Not until the Old Gangs have muddled us to catastrophe can Communists really operate; so, in the first place, the enemy is the Old Gang, and the objective is the overthrow of their power. To achieve this by constitutional means will entail at a later stage a bid for parliamentary power. In a superficial paradox, it will be necessary for a modern movement which does not believe in Parliament, as at present constituted, to seek to capture Parliament. To us, Parliament will never be an end in itself, but only a means to an end; our object is, not political place-holding, but the achievement of national reconstruction.

However, the time for elections has not yet come. First it is necessary to build a movement invading every phase of life and carrying everywhere the Corporate conception. In the first instance, we probably made a mistake in contesting parliamentary elections before we had created such a machine. It is a mistake which we have made in common with all new movements which have come to power in Europe since the War. In all cases the phase of ridicule and defeat has to be passed; indeed, it is the test of a movement's vitality. In the beginning the Old Gangs carry the day - as light-heartedly as Remus leapt over the half-built walls of Rome.

THE ATTAINMENT OF POWER

Whether our British Union of Fascists will arrive at power through the parliamentary system, or whether it will reach power in a situation far beyond the control of Parliament, no one can tell. The solution of that question will depend on two incalculable factors: (1) the rapidity with which the situation degenerates; (2) the rapidity with which the British people accept the necessity for new forms and for new organisations. If the situation develops rapidly, and the public mind develops slowly, something like collapse may come before any new movement has captured parliamentary power.

In that case, other and sterner, measures must be adopted for the saving of the State in a situation approaching anarchy. Such a situation will be none of our seeking. In no case shall we resort to violence against the forces of the Crown; but only against the forces of anarchy if, and when, the machinery of state has been allowed to drift into powerlessness. Strangely enough, such an eventuality is probably a lesser menace, when the character of the British people is considered, than the possibility of a long, slow decline which is so imperceptible that the national will to action is not aroused. In crisis the British are at their best; when the necessity for action is not clear, they are at their worst. It is possible that we may not come to any clearly marked crisis: and here arises a still greater danger. The industrial machine is running on two cylinders instead of six. A complete breakdown would be a stronger incentive to action than the movement, however cumbrous, of a crippled machine. So long as there is movement of any kind, however inadequate, there is always a lazy hope of better things. The supreme danger is that Britain may sink, almost in her sleep, to the position of a Spain - alive, in a sense, but dead to all sense of greatness and to her mission in the world.

In a situation of so many and such diverse contingencies nobody can dogmatise upon the future. We cannot say with certainty when catastrophe will come, nor whether it will take the form of a sharp crisis or of a steady decline to the status of a second-rate Power. All that we can say with certainty is that Britain cannot muddle on much longer without catastrophe, or the loss of her position in the world. Against either contingency it is our duty to arouse the nation. To meet either the normal situation of political action, or the abnormal situation of catastrophe, it is our duty to organise. Therefore, while the principles for which we fight can be clearly described in a comprehensive system of politics, of economics and of life, it would be folly to describe precisely in advance the road by which we shall attain them. A great man of action once observed: "No man goes very far who knows exactly where he is going" and the same observation applies with some force to modern movements of reality in the changing situations of today.

We ask those who join us to march with us in a great and hazardous adventure. We ask them to be prepared to sacrifice all, but to do so for no small and unworthy ends. We ask them to dedicate their lives to building in this country a movement of the modern age, which by its British expression shall transcend, as often before in our history, every precursor of the Continent in conception and in constructive achievement.

We ask them to re-write the greatest pages of British history by finding for the spirit of their age its highest mission in these islands. Neither to our friends nor to the country do we make any promises; not without struggle and ordeal will the future be won. Those who march with us will certainly face abuse, misunderstanding, bitter animosity, and possibly the ferocity of struggle and of danger. In return, we can only offer to them the deep belief that they are fighting that a great land may live.

Lightning Source UK Ltd.
Milton Keynes UK
UKOW04f0930170116

266479UK00001B/67/P